Writing *Hull*

True-life Tales from Sixteen Writers

EDITED
WITH AN INTRODUCTION BY
MARTIN GOODMAN

TYPESET BY BENJAMIN S. KAY

First published in 2012 by

BARBICAN PRESS

11 Rokel Court

Hull HU6 7TJ

Designed and typeset by Benjamin S. Kay

Photocredit: The River Hull © Martin Goodman

This work is licenced under a Creative Commons Attribution-NonCommercial-No-Derivs 3.0 Unported Licence. You are free to to copy, distribute and transmit the work under the following conditions: you must attribute the work in the manner specified by the author or licensor (but not in any way that suggests that they endorse you or your use of the work); you may not use this work for commercial purposes; you may not alter, transform, or build upon this work. This is with the understanding that: any of the above conditions can be waived if you get permission from the copyright holder; where the work or any of its elements is in the public domain under applicable law, that status is in no way affected by the licence. In no way are any of the following rights affected by the licence: your fair dealing or fair use rights, or other applicable copyright exceptions and limitations; the author's moral rights; rights other persons may have either in the work itself or in how the work is used, such as publicity or privacy rights. For any reuse or distribution, you must make clear to others the licence terms of this work.

Copyright remains with individual authors.

The production of this book was supported through funding from the Joint Information Systems Committee (JISC)

ISBN-13: 978-0-9563364-9-1

Contents

Introduction *Martin Goodman*	1
Reinventing Hull *Steve Walsh*	7
The Base of Death Hill *Chris Westoby*	19
The Tattooed Earl *Lorraine Gouland*	33
Spurn Point, September 2010 *Matthew Shaw*	41
Hilary versus Hitler *David Tomlinson*	49
Madame Clapham: a history of Hull couture *Maria Stead*	59
Humber Buildings *Mike Gower*	71
Barbarians In Rome *Nick Chapman*	77
Suicides and the Humber Bridge *Sarah Woods*	85

A View of East Yorkshire *Abby Harrison*	97
When Adam met Fat Billy *Mike Gower*	101
Hull's Royal Station Hotel & The Parapsychologist *Darren Lee Dobson*	113
Foundations *Kate Cooper*	125
What are Boyes made of? *Alison Wood*	131
Quilting the Light Fantastic *Kate Cooper*	145
Finkle Street *Amanda Bird*	149
Wilberforce, Blackburn & Sheaf *Ivor Church*	153
The Rank Outsider *Brian Lavery*	159
Hull Fair *Abby Harrison*	163
Biographies	167

Introduction

Martin Goodman

In his piece 'Rebranding Hull', Steve Walsh writes of the time marketers tagged Hull with the label 'pioneering'. On my Saturday walk from home to the KC Stadium, I wondered what label might be more fitting.

It was a solo walk at first, just me on empty pavements, but by Springbank I was part of a crowd. This was matchday. People wore the yellow and black strip of 'The Tigers', Hull City FC. They walked in groups of friends, and to a large extent as families. Football is many things to a community, but it starts with family days out. There's something sweetly tribal about it. Your team bears the name of your city and takes the field to beat all-comers. Fathers and mothers wrap up their children in team colours, scarves round their necks and hats on their heads, and shepherd them off through the cold and into the tradition. For a while I walked with them, no longer alone, part of a big family. Maybe that's a better label, I wondered—'Hull: The Family City.'

And then I swerved aside. Hull was at home to my own team, Leicester City. Hull had taken on Leicester's manager and many of its players, and Leicester had just snatched the manager back. This was a grudge match. Somewhat reluctantly I peeled away from my new Hull family and headed for the North Stand, thereby branding myself a Leicester supporter. The ticket office was not allowed to sell me a ticket, for segregation is still oddly legal in the sporting world. My only way in was to stuff bank notes through a grill to someone sitting in the gloom. A narrow turnstile of floor-to-ceiling iron bars cranked me inside. It had the deadening feeling of entering prison. All gleam and struts on the outside, as though the KC stadium were

Writing *Hull*

a giant spaceship landed in East Yorkshire, the interior strips itself back to stark functionality. Stuck in a concrete cavern, you can head to a seat, or queue for a burger and pint from the concession stands, or line up for a spot at the steel urinals. One surprising touch of daintiness comes from the handbasins in the Gents, white porcelain sized for a child and fixed low to the walls. They serve as miniature urinals for fat guys who turn their heads and beam as they stand there and hope their cleverness has been noticed.

I buy the *Hull Daily Mail*, keep abreast of football news, and have adopted Hull as my second team, but I still check the Leicester football website every morning. Grow out of it, I tell myself, but I don't choose to. My mother was an avid fan of Leicester from infancy. She owned a football rattle that was once as big as herself. Just before she died, I bought a brick with her name on that was fixed into the new stadium walls. This day at the KC shocked me though. In some ways my mother would have been familiar with the display (Leicester were clueless, gave away a penalty, had their captain sent off, and lost 2-1, so no great surprises there). The manner of the supporters, though, was not what she grew up with. Football chants can be scabrous: inventive, cutting and funny. Instead of that, oafs stood up, punched fists toward the Hull crowd, and yelled racist abuse. If you came from Hull and not Leicester, you ranked as slime, was the gist of it. These Leicester men turned to the Hull players and, in their kinder moments, wished them broken legs.

'This is disgusting,' I complained to the man on my left. Born in Leicester, he now lived in West Yorkshire. Screaming obscenities at people from East Yorkshire seemed fair enough to him. 'I live here,' I told him. 'Hull's my home.'

Kids were dancing and singing on their way from the stadium. I joined the Hull crowd as we swept toward Hessle Road, happy to merge in again.

I spent my first week in Hull in 1982. My current stay is three years and counting. I'm an outsider, though on my very first day passers-by looked me in the eye and said hello. I've brought many writers in on visits, and the adjective they most commonly use about the city is 'friendly'. That's not bad as a label, but I'm going to choose another. For all the perils of branding that Steve Walsh points out, I am going to be brazen. Here's my label: 'Hull: The Storytelling City.'

No city has invested in storytelling as much as Hull. I don't simply mean in literature, though from Marvell through Larkin to now we have a world-class pedigree in which even poetry is focused on storytelling. What I mean by storytelling is the recognition that the land, its seas and its people all have dramas and life-cycles that weave around each other. The region is forged by its stories.

So how has Hull invested in this? There's the Hull History Centre for a start, a landmark building set into the heart of the city. It merges the archives of city and university, and core to its mission is the encouragement of locals to come in, discover, and learn to tell their stories. The Deep is a storytelling venture, spiralling visitors down into a submarium as they learn of the interplay between humans and the seas. The Maritime Museum tells the story of seafaring, while history in the Museum Quarter stretches back beyond Roman mosaics to a Bronze-age boat some 4000 years old.

Hull is a great survivor. Given the whole-scale wartime blitz, surplus bombs dumped on the city before planes retreated across the North Sea, the fact that so much quality remains in the winding streets of the Old Town is remarkable. Close on miraculous for me is Trinity Square, dominated by the beauty of Holy Trinity Church and with the old 16th Century grammar school attended by the likes of Andrew Marvell and William Wilberforce tucked into its corner. Those buildings remain while so much else was smashed from existence. I see Hull as the great survivor for that spirit which sees it pick itself up, dust itself down, and reinvent itself. Such rallying happened after its wartime bombing, after the loss of its fishing industry, after the recent floods. Low-lying and set beside the North

Sea, the region is set to receive the brunt of climate change, already evidenced by flooding and the depletion of fish stocks in the North Sea. Faced with the challenges of global economic downturn, Hull is likely to continue to top many lists of social deprivation statistics. The narrative of Hull, reshaping its identity to confront new challenges, contains lessons and experiences well worth sharing with the world. Why might this be particularly true of Hull? Globally, the notion of a consumerist society fuelled by perpetual growth is being challenged. That is not the prevailing attitude in Hull and the region. This is not a get-rich-quick culture. What comes may likely go. What abides is a sense of history, of continuation, of landscape and community. These are core values and they can be imparted through story.

In this collection, David Tomlinson introduces us to Hilary. Now an old lady, Hilary looks down from the heights of the Wolds to recall the wartime era of her childhood when Hull was the most blitzed city after London. From the vantage points of both height and old age, she passes comment on the way we live now. Pubs remain natural storytelling venues, as well as pick-up joints. The sign creaks in the winds that blow by the closed Earl de Grey on Castle Street, but the pub finds life in the tale told by Lorraine Gouland. It's tough being a young woman in the merchant navy. This story is stoked with real characters and telling details that take us in to that alien world.

In my first children's event for the Philip Larkin Centre, children brought in storyboards through which they had recounted their experiences of the recent floods. When your home and your school are swept away, when everything that made up your family home is replaced by filth, and when you squeeze with others into a caravan for months on end, it's a lot to process. Story helps to do it. In this collection you will find moments of life rendered raw and touched with loss, turned tender in the telling.

True-life Tales from Sixteen Writers

The writers in this book all took part in Hull University's MA in Creative Writing, and these pieces stem from a module in creative nonfiction. What is creative nonfiction? Well, this is. This collection shows off the form very well. Writers sniff material – it might be in the look of a building, a statistic in a newspaper, an anecdote overheard, a memory that wakes itself up – and then go rooting for more facts. This might mean taking a walk, interviewing someone, digging through archives, or staring through a window while further memories surface. And then comes the creative part. The trick here is to go beyond a simple record of the facts. To tell a story well, you need to conjure the reader into a sense of being there as the action unfolds. That means choosing the lively storyline, and also researching the details that give juice to it. What were the smells and sounds like? What was the quality of light as it moved across a landscape? Who were the characters and how did they speak? The pieces here have been polished by writers working well to develop their craft, so that the experiences of others become your own as you read.

You can be driving along a city street in Hull, and what seems some arbitrary border is crossed. While nothing obvious has changed, you have left the city and entered the East Riding. Boundaries blur still more as Hull spills into Cottingham, which claims its own definition as the largest village in England. Hull was the one city within an area known as Humberside until 1996, stretching beyond Beverley and over the Humber to North Lincolnshire. Now it is its own authority but a part of East Yorkshire. It has a separate history wrapped up in an alternative name, Kingston on Hull. Given that fluid sense of identity and naming and belonging, it is natural for this book to reflect the wider region. The department store Boyes feels central to Hull's Hessle Road, but Alison Wood traces its story for us back through Bridlington to an interview with a family member still guiding the stores from Scarborough. Stand on the North

Bank of the Humber and you can look south toward Barton, but a tale such as Chris Westoby's lets you cross the bridge and live a whole slice of Barton life as your own. People are swept away by the river, and Sarah Woods gives us insights into such sad dramas. We'll take you to Spurn Point, through a fire-ravaged building, stand and admire as parents whirl across the dance floor, and go looking for history that is hidden in the city's architecture. We write of Hull because all life is here. These are chapters in an ongoing story.

Just before kick-off at the KC Stadium, as the winter sky darkened, a pair of swans flew high above the pitch. 30,000 people gathered around the floodlit grass below them, but the whole scene was just an instant in the journey of the swans' lives. That vision of swans in flight illuminates an understanding that is important to nonfiction writing—the fact that nothing can be seen as being apart from its environment. A football match can be captured by statistics, and a life summarised by a list of its accomplishments, but both are impoverished versions. Choose a subject for a biography and then what must open out for you are the places that person passed through, the people with whom they entered into relationship, the financial difficulties and cultural challenges, perhaps even the weather that prompted a particular shift in the order of that person's life on a particular day. Of course as soon as the writer chooses to write about something, that very attention and the writer's presence has an impact on the situation they are observing.

Many writers here have chosen to include themselves in their story, and some have not. These stories now have the chance to come alive in readers' imaginations. Material picked up from one tale by readers will feed into their experience of another. Some pieces here have already prompted me to break from reading and travel out so as to stand and walk where the stories first took me. I have further outings planned. I'll see you there, maybe.

Reinventing Hull

Steve Walsh

My three-year-old son's asleep in the back of the car, dreaming about knights and dragons, so I've got time. I wait for the sparse Sunday traffic to pass. Then I point and press. The camera does its little digital sneeze and I thumb the review button. The picture's OK, a bit grainy. The main thing is, the wording on the sign's legible: 'Welcome to Kingston upon Hull,' it says. 'The Pioneering City.'

The Pioneering City – what does that mean? When people talk about Hull, outsiders, I mean – and they do sometimes – they'll probably mention: fishing, John Prescott, Hull City, rugby league, The Housemartins, Crap Towns, Hull, Hell and Halifax. If they're more knowledgeable, if they've read a travel piece in *The Guardian*, say, they might have heard about the white phone boxes and the poetic connection with Marvell and Larkin; they might know that the city used to be the country's largest deep sea fishing port; that it once turned away an autocratic king from its gates; that it was the forgotten 'North-East coastal town' of the Second World War news reels. If their go-to news source has a different agenda, they'll know the city as a hell of unwanted housing and bad schools, with teenage mums and drug addicts running amok.

But what does this sign have to do with all this? Standing sentinel on a central reservation at Hull's northern boundary, where 1960s tower blocks give way all at once to fields and electricity pylons, its meaning is obscure. Like one of those old faded brick wall adverts for long-vanished brands of boot black or high tar cigarettes, only the slogan remains. But, just over a decade ago, this phrase, 'the pioneering city', was coined to encompass everything positive about Hull. And the people hated it.

Turning on the cog

It's February 2000 and strange things are happening in Hull. Over three days, the Hull Daily Mail has received more than 200 letters of complaint. For once, they're not banging on about bin collections or bus services but a work of graphic design, known universally as 'the cog'. The city's new logo is a complete waste of money, they say, an affront to civic traditions. Not only that, with its lower case 'h' for 'hull', it's ungrammatical.

For some people, words are not enough. They want to trample all over it. When a city centre floral display depicting the symbol is unveiled, they get their chance. Hundreds of pansies are left for dead.

When a new universal identity for Hull was first mooted in the late 1990s, the city was undergoing a makeover. After over a decade of stagnation following the demise of the fishing industry in the 1970s, things seemed to be happening again. In the evocative words of the then council leader, Patrick Doyle, there were once again 'cranes on the skyline'.

Alongside the physical regeneration, funded by the European Union and central government, a concerted effort was being made to upgrade Hull's image too. The city would no longer be seen as an economically and socially deprived port. In the optimistic spirit of New Labour's 'third way', it would be recast as a 'top ten' city. Former grain warehouses on the River Hull would now be home to minimalist office spaces for burgeoning creative and 'knowledge-based' industries. 'Celebrating the past, pioneering the future' went the slogan coined by Hull's new marketing gurus.

They justified Hull's new USP with a post-modern mix grabbed from culture and history. The turning away of King Charles I from the town walls at the start of the English Civil Wars was one example, the invention of liquid crystals by researchers at the University of Hull another. From these disparate elements, they forged a new identity, 'the pioneering city'.

That offensive 'cog' logo, with its five 'teeth', was meant to represent the different facets of Hull's pioneering spirit: leading, creating, challenging, discovering and innovating. Even the city's name was finessed. Ever since the granting of its first Royal Charter in 1299 when Wyke upon Hull was renamed King's Town, Hull has had a fraught relationship with its regal appendage. The branders came definitively down on the side of the single-syllable form, which should, they said, appear on all the signs welcoming visitors on the city's approach roads as well as on maps and public transport timetables.

Around this time, I'd just landed my first proper job – as a copywriter with a local PR agency. As well as spinning company newspaper stories about new factory packing lines and shy secretaries with a fondness for decorating eggs, I found myself involved in marketing the 'new Hull'. Which is how, on February 3rd, 2000, I came to have a ringside seat at Hull's New Theatre for the brand's glitzy launch.

My main recollection of the evening, apart from the spectacle of marketing types doing their tribal greetings of air kisses and high fives, was an unscripted heckle.

Behind his Plexiglas pulpit, Cityimage chief executive John Till was reaching the emotive crescendo of his speech.

"If we all take on the job of being ambassadors for our pioneering brand, consistently and in everything we do… we can build a brighter future for everyone in this city."

Then a small voice piped up from the audience:

"Not with that little 'h' you won't."

It was like the mortifying moment in the film, *Spinal Tap*, when the tiny Stonehenge prop descends from on high. But to me and many others, there was a more fundamental problem with the brand than its 'little h'.

In the marketing publications I helped produce, we were forever describing a Hull that didn't really exist. Initiatives were always 'about to' bear fruit; an employment scheme 'could' provide benefits; a new landmark building was 'set to' transform the skyline. The stories overlooked the complexities of the present to concentrate on a bright future that was always, tantalisingly, just around the corner.

Partial truths like these served to undermine the brand's credibility. One blogger commented: "People will not feel positive about their city when they live in sub-standard housing, when they feel unsafe in their own homes, when they are constantly reminded about how their children are failing in school and when traditional jobs and livelihoods have vanished."

The branding experts didn't help their case by piling on the hype. Talk of altering 'the DNA of Hull to make ourselves one of the country's top 10 cities' only seemed to remind those living here how far the reality fell short of the image.

Dr David Atkinson, a cultural and historical geographer at the University of Hull, believes the notion of trying to be a high-profile, world-class city modelled on London or Manchester was misconceived.

"Hull's never going to reach those kinds of levels," he told me over a cup of tea in the University's Arts Cafe. "If you chase after that and it doesn't happen, it risks undermining the whole process of getting people to think of Hull as a place to invest and live in."

Although not opposed to the idea of place branding per se, David has criticised the way the marketing of Hull glossed over important elements of the city's industrial heritage, such as its whaling and fishing industries, because they didn't fit in with branders' ideas of what a 21st century city should look like.

"Whaling and fishing are a crucial part of what Hull's all about," he said. "Omitting these things because of their supposedly dubious reputation is short-sighted, particularly for people associated with the fishing community. They feel excluded."

In 2007, ignored and unloved, Hull's brand was, quietly, dumped.

Of course, this wasn't how everyone saw it. John Till, Cityimage's former chief executive, now runs a marketing agency specialising in place branding.

"Place branding is still very new," he told me over the phone. "Twelve years ago, when we worked on Hull, it didn't exist at all. Nobody had done it. We were making it up as we went along.

"It's not about producing a logo. We don't even tend to use the word branding. We talk about the story of a place. Branding conjures up images of blokes with pony tails."

Unfairly or not, this was precisely how many Hull people viewed the city's image makers in the early years of the 21st century. They were interlopers playing fast and loose with the city's heritage for the sake of a nifty logo. John acknowledges that mistakes were made.

"I think part of the problem was that [the cog] became the focus point. At the launch, we talked for an hour and about [the cog] for only two minutes. But it got all the focus. I think if you're going to go for visual messages, you have to do it more softly."

Still, he remains bullish about the brand's overall legacy. The Deep, an angular modernist aquarium overlooking the Humber, has been a big draw for visitors since it opened in 2001. But, says John, this and other new 'landmark' buildings only commanded such high-quality designs because of the 'top 10 city' aspirations championed by the brand. It also provided simple, positive messages – a weapon to counter the vilification of Hull that's never far away.

'Flat and nice for cycling'

Hull never seems to get a good press. In the early 2000s, Crap Towns, a toilet book about – well, have a guess – rubbished Hull's attempts to reinvent itself. A couple of years later, Channel 4's *Location, Location* did much the same for its reputation as a desirable place to live, splicing images of city centre developments with shots of dog turds.

And even when they're not deliberately setting out to slander the city, national journalists' patronising and sneering attitudes to Hull are palpable. In 2010, a new visitor attraction was launched in Hull to commemorate the 25th anniversary of Philip Larkin's death. Linking some of the sites that were significant in his work and life, the Larkin Trail might at least have prompted a deeper interest in the environment of one of Britain's most controversial post-War poets. Instead, report after report quoted Larkin's famous dismissal of the city: 'It's flat and very nice for cycling.'

In the face of outsiders' derision, it's hard sometimes to avoid becoming a caricature of the 'chippy Northerner'. In November 2011, BBC Radio Humberside morning presenter David Burns and his BBC London counterpart, Vanessa Feltz, clashed over a report that Croydon Council in London was considering relocating some of its tenants to Hull. Sidelining the main issue – the parlous state of social housing in Britain's capital – Feltz had concentrated on the lifestyle angle. How were cosmopolitan Cockneys, she mused, supposed to adapt to life in a culture-less, economically depressed North?

"I hear you've been having a pop," said Burnsy, weighing in for Hull in a live link-up between the two stations. "Well, we're puffing our chests out. We're going to be Britain's centre of renewable energy. And we don't riot up here."

I almost spat out my coffee. It was the sort of thing you heard on the football terraces, not the radio. But at the same time I could understand why he said it.

Spinning turbines

Now the need to 'correct' Hull's image is no longer just an issue of civic pride. It's about economic survival.

Hull is being badly hit in the current economic downturn. According to figures from the Centre for Cities, in November 2011, it had the highest percentage of people receiving Jobseekers Allowance in the country, as well as the largest number of claimants per job vacancy.

In keeping with the austerity of the times, Hull's current image makers no longer talk about the city's 'pioneering spirit'. Instead, Hull Bondholders, a network of local businesses, are focusing on the city's 'economic story' in a bid to attract investment and jobs.

Three of the story's four themes – Hull's connection to water, its entrepreneurial spirit and global outlook – draw on well-established features of the town's 700-year history as a trading port. The fourth, however, is much newer. Hull isn't the only city in the country pinning its hopes on a boom in renewable energy to get out of the economic doldrums. However, the Humber's proximity to one of the largest planned offshore wind farms in Europe at Dogger Bank and the availability of cheap labour here have, for once, made the region favourite to capitalise on the anticipated growth of the sector.

At the Hull Bondholders' Christmas get-together in an Old Town bar, the mood is upbeat. German energy giant, Siemens, has just announced plans for a £230m wind turbine factory in Hull's Alexandra Dock. It's expected to create around 800 jobs and, hopefully, thousands more through its supply chains.

I've come along to see if I can speak to someone involved in 'selling' Hull but networking has never come naturally to me. It feels like a nervy, corporate form of flirtation. As you juggle fiddly canapés and complimentary drinks, you find yourself slyly checking out people's name badges, seeing which company they're with, trying to think of an opener that doesn't sound too gauche. Above all, you have to look confident, never lost or alone. There must be easier ways to get a free drink.

I'm about to nip outside for another cigarette with the bouncer when someone rescues me and introduces me to Alistair Latham.

"I think you were in the year above me at school," he says. And, for once, I'm glad the usual six degrees of separation don't apply in Hull.

Alistair is an employment lawyer. Away from his day job, he is a roving ambassador for Hull Bondholders and recently took part in a trade mission to Poland. His insider knowledge is compelling.

"The Poles are really positive," he says. "They can see the opportunities here. Unlike in the rest of Europe, there's a lot of liquidity in their banks and they're looking for somewhere to spend their money. So we go over there and say: 'Don't go to London. Come to Hull.' And they're interested. Before we went, they hadn't even heard of us."

He thinks that the Hull Bondholders' focus on the commercial potential of the region, with its well-developed transport infrastructure and ports, is just right.

"We could try promoting Hull as a great destination for dining out or shopping," he says. "But what's the point? Places like York and Leeds already do that far better than we do. What we've got is a strong industrial base. If we can promote that, then that creates the wealth for people to spend money in restaurants and shopping centres further down the line."

If I'm honest, I'm slightly disappointed that image making these days is such a low-key, sensible affair. I'd looked forward to meeting some bombastic bullshitter, banging on about 'singing from the same hymn sheet' and calling me 'mate' every ten seconds. Unfortunately, all the Hull Bondholders seem quite down to earth, anxious to keep Hull's image grounded in reality. Or maybe the spin is just more subtle these days.

Even as the Bondholders embark on the latest attempt to 'reposition' Hull, traces of the pioneering city still remain.

Steve Mathie, proprietor of 'Spin It' records in Hull's indoor market, claims he started his Wall of Fame to attract more people to his stall, not to evoke some abstract branding concept. But looking around at the 160 or so individually framed profiles of Hull's famous (and not so famous) alumni that line the walls next to his racks of rare vinyl and vintage pop paraphernalia, it's hard not to make the connection with the original Hull brand. The potted histories of politicians and sportsmen, musicians and inventors read like character sketches for an epic retelling of Hull's past.

All the usual suspects are here – like aviator Amy Johnson and slavery abolitionist William Wilberforce. And with Steve's interest in music, it's natural that Mick Ronson, David Bowie's collaborator in his Ziggy Stardust phase, and David Whitfield, the first artist to have a gold record on both sides of the Atlantic, should have found their way on to the walls. But there are also tributes to Hull's three Victoria Cross recipients as well, and plenty of interesting snippets about the bit parts played by Hull people in some of the great events of history. I never realised that Hull's MPs had been present at the signing of the peace treaty at the end of the American War of Independence, or that one of New Zealand's first prime ministers was born here.

"People are always having a go at Hull," he said. "Even just the name: 'Ull. It makes us a target even though there are far worse places. People bring visitors around and they're proud to show them who's from Hull. And with young people, it shows what you can achieve, even if you are from Hull."

Civic self-esteem – it's always been in short supply in Hull. Although many who come to the city for work or study decide to stay on, Hull people themselves often can't see the qualities in their home city that are obvious to outsiders. For some reason, we're not like Liverpudlians or Geordies. We don't counter the patronising attitudes of outsiders with a fierce identity of our own. But then again, there's no Hull equivalent to 'professional Scousers' like Cilla Black or Jimmy Tarbuck. So maybe it's not all bad news.

When I left home at the age of 18 to study Biology at the University of Oxford, I missed Hull terribly. Everyone I met at college seemed so eager to fit in and move on, to leave their pasts behind. I was amazed at how quickly they threw themselves into the 'Oxford experience'. Even the Northerners I knew seemed to develop a sudden enthusiasm for punting and rowing. I hated it.

On a weekend visit home, dragging my bag full of dirty washing out the front of Paragon Station the sight of the House of Fraser in all its bleached concrete glory almost made me cry.

Here was a proper city.

If I'd followed the usual Oxford career path, gone to London, got a high-flying media job, I'd probably be an inveterate poster on internet forums and message threads by now, waxing nostalgic about the price of cocktails in Spiders nightclub or wondering whether the Hull City's latest signing could ever fill Deano's boots. But I didn't. I came home and, following the path of least resistance, ended up writing glossy versions of someone else's – some outsider's – vision of my home city. There's no danger of me crying in front of department stores any more. But it doesn't mean I don't care how Hull is represented.

Lies, damned lies and marketing

It's another autumn Sunday and I've come to a playing field in North Hull. Beresford Park has changed quite a bit since I played here as a kid in the 1970s. It no longer looks like a dilapidated Soviet-era training camp, complete with lethal steel gymnastic rings. And that roundabout I once fell off at high speed has, happily, been consigned to the Museum of Dangerous Rides.

There's something else. My son's playing pirates with his grandma on the new, health and safety-approved climbing frame. In the background, the blades of a huge wind turbine suck and slice at the air. Petrochemicals company, Croda, installed the 125-metre high structure in 2008 and now this benign landmark, the second tallest building in Hull, is visible all over the city.

It would make a great picture for a Hull Bondholders brochure – the little boy playing while the symbol of his city's future prosperity looms up overhead. Or maybe I've just spent too long thinking about branding.

If the idea of reinventing a whole city seems like hubris to us now, the original 'pioneering city' project should perhaps be seen in its historical context. For the 1990s and early 2000s was the era when the brand came of age. It was the time when global corporations lost any residual shred of self-restraint, using any opportunity to push their identities and 'consolidate' their market position. The logos for Starbucks, Nike, McDonalds and Apple became as ubiquitous as road signs. Also, with the growth of the brand came the rise of the public relations industry, which experienced soaring revenues between 1990 and 2000.

All of these factors came together in the reinvention of Hull. Wally Olins, the creative consultant hired to supply Hull's new identity, has subsequently spoken of a place's brand as being nothing more than a distillation of its reputation. Just as Paris has become known, through a long history of cultural association, as the city of love, so Hull could become, in the public imagination, the city of pioneers.

Marketing specialists would have us believe that this process of reinvention is more necessary now than ever, as cities and indeed whole regions have to compete for scarce funding, investment and tourist pounds.

But, in my view, this partial telling of Hull's story also reinforces a sense of inferiority. By having to appeal to the outside world and adapt our 'product' to satisfy it, we risk not only denigrating our own self-worth but also undermining the very thing that makes us distinctive and vital in the first place.

I don't know if there'll be any jobs in renewable energy when my son Tom leaves school in 15 years. I hope so. But whether the wealth created by the industry will be enough to revive the region's fortunes is a different matter. Hull has been a prosperous city in the past but its social problems – poor housing, low educational attainment and limited career opportunities – have been with us in good times and bad. So while it's understandable that the local council and businesses should spin the good news of the Siemens investment for all they're worth, it's going to take more than that to pull the city out of the worst recession since the Second World War. Personally, I doubt the political will is there; it's so much easier (and cheaper) to come up with a new marketing strap line.

Right now, Tom's interested in other types of stories, mainly ones involving superheroes, monsters and rockets. But if a lack of opportunity forces him to leave the city of his birth in the coming years, his last view of it might well be a road sign in the rearview mirror: 'Welcome to Hull, The Pioneering City'.

The Base of Death Hill

Chris Westoby

We escape down the stairs and into the carpark, the fermented aftertaste of underage drinking still alien to us. We walk in the dark, feeling like giants. The Dead Semester gig had been a tumble dryer of swirling, pounding, pushing, shouting, ringing.

'Fucking terrible,' I laugh, sounding too loud in the streets. 'He sounded like Sylvester Stallone. He kept going he's my father.'

'He's my farder,' Matt slur-shouts.

'-e's my farder,' I echo.

And then together: 'Blerr der ma nerr ner ner.'

'He should have gone all the way and shouted Adrian, I did it!' I say.

We head away from Barton, up the crop field skirting Death Hill, where we once played human skittles using big motorway cones; where I once ate that crop and got ill; where Conner accidentally picked up dog shit. The trees where we found that brown-stained bed and used it for a sledge. That den under the bank where I first reached under a girl's clothes.

Death Hill's called Death Hill because someone died there. It's that steep, fifty meter slope, down from the motorway, with the concrete ditch at the bottom. Someone once went down on a bike and couldn't stop before the ditch - blood everywhere. Bollocks, I say. But I do know someone else set up a ramp and cleared it. Probably on a different day. We would speed down Death Hill on traffic cones. I once did her in under four seconds and got thirteen thistle splinters in my palms. Someone once set the whole thing on fire.

We reach the top of the field.

Up here, you're afforded a view of Barton no one really cares to observe, the best one. You look down a slope of black nothing to where the town starts. Street lights scatter like glitter, clustering to a gold horizon beyond. You hear the motorway traffic somewhere over the bank, heading way out over the Humber Bridge there, those two columns of red lights, the dot-to-dot arc of streetlights, the red and gold streaming over it. Hessle's that last line of lights, barely visible. Barton is always growing outwards into farms and fields like this one. Fourteen year old me doesn't know, but I'm probably in someone's future living room right now.

Crouched within some cauliflowers, we use our colour phone screens for light whilst trying to roll Samson cigarettes.

'Here, look.' My finished effort resembles a witchetty grub.

Matt takes a pull and passes it back. He stands up and watches a car pass, a quarter-mile away. 'Not a soul knows we're here.'

Somewhere down the field, past all those lights, our friends wonder where we are.

'Here's what we've got to do.' I pan a finger across Barton. 'Your house is, like...there. We've got to get to it as the crow flies. In a straight line. In that direction. Through gardens, alleyways, whatever. Even if there's a dog.' My Samson bobs between my lips as I speak. 'And no one can see us.' We time our breaks across open lawns, over gates and through gardens. Under windows and through hedges. We climb a summerhouse and jump a larger wall. 'This is a doctor's place,' Matt whispers, after half an hour of stealth. We're in a queer, huge garden. Fragments of patio litter an overgrown lawn; there's a deep pit I can't see to the bottom of; palm trees flap their wings in slow-motion. A firework goes off somewhere. The sky pulses green, then black again. 'So?'

'Just. Don't know. His wife's got cancer and he looks after her all day. Even if he saw us, he probably wouldn't come out.'

'Why are you saying this?'

Barton's dangerous. Maybe it got worse as I grew up, or maybe it's a side I only saw once the adult haunts became available, like your first time watching TV after 9pm.

Primary school was a bubble of innocence.

Secondary school had wagered fights behind the sports hall with steel chains, and half once got burned to the ground.

It was all about gangs, fighting and marking territory with acronyms. Caistor Road Elite (CRE). The New Holland Crew (NHC is scrawled even on my leavers book). Ramsden Ave Crew (un-caring that RAC was already taken). You learn about drug deals being made. What that single firework above Barton View means.

And before you're eighteen, the floodgates open: people are being stabbed, beaten into comas, attacked in a park, bottled; shops are bullied into shut-down, houses smashed through. You hear about the guy whose brain inside his lead-piped head was swelling so fast that his skull had to be opened. What kids did to that disabled man on West Acridge. The elderly, the vulnerable, the young. Broken limbs. Scars.

People you know involved, not all of them victims.

But there are sections you can escape to; I learned better than most. When seventeen and overwhelmed by a disorder, Barton's edges were the unclimbable fences of my enclosure. I never left. Unable to attend college, unable to face home, I walked about, most of the day, most days, for a year and a half. As far from eyes as possible. I knew a few places. Let me show you one.

Out the back of a nature reserve, in the thickly-spun brambles and berry trees, among the tight muddy paths you shoulder through, you happen across a hidden graveyard of old buildings. Impractically designed red brickworks, belonging to no one but the roots pulling them down. You trip on the odd concrete wall laying under nettles, or spot a whole blueprint of foundations in a clearing, holding reeds and water like abandoned swimming baths. And then the trees end and all these ruins spill down a beach.

This was where I'd come hide.

You see the Humber Bridge thrown across the river to your right,

Hessle peeking out the North bank trees, the train running beside the Clive Sullivan. You're stood on shingles like ice-cream sprinkles. Chalk, flint, broken tiles. Tall wooden support beams protrude from the silt, rusted bolts working their way free of the rotten grain. Cement floors the size of your living room are turned erect by the Humber, brown water farting through the little caves and corridors they form. Concrete banks still hold the shape and print of the hessian bags they were laid in. Old sewage pipes poke out the bank and leak. Look at this thing: a cuboid of bricks about my height, four foot wide, on a base of its own uprooted foundations like a big Subbuteo piece.

People say different things about these relics. Some that it was an old jetty used by smugglers between Barton and Hull; others say between Barton and New Holland, a few miles up the Humber; others say between Barton and regular Holland, a few miles further. It was a tile factory. It was an industrial waste dump. No, it was just a pier; they used it in the war to carry supplies. It fell into disrepair. It was bombed. Got shut down. Went out of business. Hell, I don't want to know the true purpose.

This place speaks volumes about we Bartonians, I think, throwing a finely crafted skimming stone over the silt and into the Humber. None of us can account for a place this big sitting right on our door step, but we all know about the boy who bit someone's little finger off outside the Water Margin on Christmas Eve.

I came down here on the second winter of being town-bound and found that a huge square the size of three football fields had been blown out the shore, like a giant had stomped his spade into the bank and hauled. The beach you could once walk all the way to South Ferriby now trailed as a miniature Spurn Point into oiled mud or high tide for two hundred meters until the beach continued. A bench faced the gulf, as though it was something to admire. I tried to cross the waist-deep slop by hopping the rocks.

Returning brings a strange sensation; awful memories rewired into something nostalgic. I'm twenty one and it's summer. The slab of silt is a hard-baked and cracked miniature desert; I walk easily across. As kids, my brothers and me used to collect iron we found amongst the chalk and flint, the corroded guts of vessels, and make a stash hidden in reeds. Probably somewhere around here, I think, tapping dry silt with my sole. It's a rare place of peace.

You see, in the last five years, Barton council have cottoned on to the brownie points we can gain from flaunting our position beside the estuary, locking down every last rabbit hole as precious 'reserved' nature, so long as you can see a glimpse of the Humber Bridge nearby. If the rarest Icterine Warbler's nest doesn't have a photo-worthy backdrop of the bridge behind it, you can approach them with your peri-peri sauce at the ready for all the council care. But I don't mind the ugly info centres and wooden duck-spying huts behind every bush. Barton has to capitalize on what it's got.

For example, the RopeWalk was formerly an extraordinarily long factory established in the eighteenth century; it fabricated the rope used by the first man to scale Everest, and later used machinery designed by my grandfather. But times moved on. So in the new millennium, after a decade of being abandoned, it was renovated into an art gallery. This would be great, were it not for the scandal that the rear studios were being used to film pornography. A Bartonian debate: which of the two mediums were making more money? Which owns the better masterpiece?

Sharing the carpark is Tesco, the true symbol of a changing town. Proudfoot (now revered as some saint of cheaper cooked chicken) was ousted by the throat. Tesco made an offer for their not-for-sale premises. If they refused, Tesco would build their own building anyway, within a mile, running it out of business entirely. Proudfoot wisely took the former option. Our local high street of grocers, butchers and off-licenses were not afforded the same offer. What was once the hub of business here is being washed of customers by the convenience and confoundingly good prices of Tesco.

We'd like to say we stood against it all, but integrity can't hold a torch to logic. When the old martyrs got a taste for aisle shopping, where hopping from groceries to electronics didn't mean crossing a cold street, they chose the warm. Personally, I don't care much that the little people are being squashed; it's about time the commercial side woke up and smelt the money. Barton is growing faster than our narrow high streets and one-way roads can accommodate. We are bursting at the seams, reaching out with pale housing estates and almost touching our neighbouring villages. Successful young couples are moving into the outskirts with Audis and Chihuahuas. By comparison, Barton's centre seems old, like the rotten core, and we all want out.

Beer garden conversation between folks my age on a night out are plans to find better places, as though Barton's a grotty kindergarten you need to escape. You finish a rant and look behind you, through the smeary glass, to the dance floor, where a group of divorcees are rubbing each other up. You look between your mates' shoulders to the table across from you, where the cool kids from school, the bullies, are now on the wrong side of twenty five, living at home, losing their hair, wasting their money on Carling and Xbox games.

There are, I count, almost twenty pubs in Barton, and they're shutting down. Juggling from one owner to the next like hot potatoes as they drain of customers, income, alcohol. Shaped by the people living here. The ones which heave like an ant nest are those which try to be a club. Charlie's, The Swan, Coach and Horses, Red Lion, The George Hotel, were all ordinary pubs; but now the lights are out, the floor sticky, the music distortedly coughing up Capital FM's top ten, the smell potent and sweet, mafting hot, the bartenders angry, the beer fizzier than lemonade. Eyes meeting yours everywhere. Toilets where your feet splash in the piss if you walk too heavily, yet someone'll be laid out there marinating. Black mould hanging from the ceiling, as though even the building's caught an

STI. These places serve food in the day. Smokers shiver outside without knowing they're cold. The odd fight snaps between two boys with too much gel in their hair. The odd pull between a twenty and fifty year old.

Ask my friend John about that. We walked out the George last winter; it was two o'clock, the air was frozen, and John was teaching me to be single again - by example, apparently. A taxi door popped and the midlife inside squawked 'You coming?' I'd no idea if they'd met inside earlier. Only that John's night later involved running two miles, ushering children to bed, and a bird of prey. I forget the order.

If you are timid, you'll be trampled. And if you're male, keep your hair under an inch long. I once got started on by a frail looking man who waited until he had four others to support him. A guy once spilt their drink over their hand, turned to me and wiped it on my best top. I spat on my hand and wiped it on him. John got his head smashed on a wall last spring because they mistook him for someone else. I'd get free quadruple vodkas snuck from our friend tending bar, a favour he called when it got closed down and he wanted me to help steal the fag machine. But lighten up. You can either feel rotten for stepping foot in a place like this, or you can wallow in the mud.

I'm twenty, in that beer garden; we're at the end of a pub-golf night, all dressed up accordingly. It's ten minutes until John's head is smashed. He's inside, somewhere.

'Why does everyone think they're better than here?' I ask the group. 'Because it's Barton,' says Shaun. 'The cities're where the money's at. Can't wait to be gone, man. Shit hole. My brother's moved to Leeds with his girlfriend, making over twenty a year already. Alicia's in Blackpool with a shit-hot job. Man, it's where it's at. Anywhere but here. I want to go into recruitment, in London. Live with young professionals. Eventually be a manager.'

'What's recruitment?'

'Recruitment.'

'Right,' I sit my head on my hand; it gets so heavy when I'm drunk. The door bangs open, the music within momentarily loud; Joshua is led past by a bouncer and thrown out the gate.

John comes out and shrugs dramatically.

'What happened?' I laugh.

He shrugs again and sits down, sweaty. 'Tried it on with someone's wife, I reckon. He-'

A little explosion and the scatter of glass sounds from behind the fence.

'Shit.' John gets up. People are squeezing to look through the gate. The landlord's brand new Volkswagen has a smashed rear window, and I'll later learn that Joshua managed to limp-run home with a severely fractured leg. The landlord is backed by umpteen baldies, and they all want blood. Stalking round the car, chests out, going who the fuck was it? Our little group sticks out like cardigan and flat-cap-clad accomplices.

I pine for the time before I was born, when our precious pinch of 'pub pubs' or 'old man pubs' thrived. Not adhering to the growing demand for playhouses has left most out of business, today. The beer's good; the food's good. They've barred the last honest alcoholics Barton has left.

Are they mad?

A distant uncle of mine would have a taxi booked to be outside the Wheatsheaf every weeknight ready to ferry him home, blind-drunk, every night, for fifteen years. That's surely a loyal customer. Non-conformity isn't rewarded in Barton. We're like Emperor Penguins: stand out from the crowd and you'll only freeze to death.

You do what you can to stay open. There was a time you could walk past even the George and see a few old ladies having pub lunch, crinkling their noses at the taste.

My nan attempted food there, three years ago.

'The table and floor were sticky, and the waitress had black teeth. She stunk like a bag of fish' was her review.

Okay, there are places to eat that wouldn't fail a Chlamydia screen. Elio's is an Italian with delicious food; the head chef comes out to check on you, wearing pyjama bottoms. The Surma is a stellar Indian, and with twenty free handshakes from the staff, picking up a takeaway feels like accepting a lifetime achievement award. Mamma Mia's staff of two ashy dumplings sit on the door-step and smoke all day. Pizza Jim lets beautiful girls look behind the counter. Whatever that means. Barton Grill opened when I was sixteen, and within a fortnight closed down temporarily because, reputedly, the health and safety folk found an illegal immigrant boy in one of the kitchen cupboards.

What else do we have?

We have a 'cursed' building that's seen scores of new businesses start and end like mayflies. There's a huge house near the park where, apparently, there's the entrance to an underground tunnel eight miles long which runs all the way to Thornton Abby. There's a little house no one's lived in since a man murdered his family there. A tree grows from within it now, out the windows and gaps in the walls.

Robert Elmer Kleason, whose methods of dismembering the people he murdered was said to have influenced The Texas Chainsaw Massacre (1974), lived here, and was taught to drive by my friend's father.

I walked home from football training when I was nine, in broad daylight, and down a street adjacent to where I walked a man stood on a low wall with his trousers pulled down; a woman was facing him, stood on the path, holding his waist, pressing her face into his groin. It was a while before I learned what that was. There's a carnival once a year. We used to have giant floats, motorbike and eagle shows, clowns throwing goodie bags into the crowd like flank steaks to hyenas. I won a fish at a hook-a-duck there that lasted eight years, and ate our prize Shubunkin. We had the Crazy Shake, a sixty-foot disk with only a bench around the edges that spun faster and faster, and then tipped up forty-five degrees like the sinking Titanic and flicked people down. Damn health and safety to hell for banning that.

There used to be a Christmas festival too, but not anymore. I think someone died.

St. Peter's church is on the map, but no one notices it above you when you round that high-walled corner near the train station where someone reputedly Spartan-kicked an NHC tyke off the platform. St. Mary's is the one that's used. Someone I knew lost their virginity in the graveyard. The vicar's called Half Pint. Our local Cyprian barber's funeral filled the church, the graveyard, and the surrounding road. Some people are truly loved.

I'd walk in to his barber shop as a child, as my father did, and no matter what you asked him to do, he'd say '...So you wanna haircut?!'. Old men sat around the edge smoking and reading the smut off the coffee table. No barber since has dared to trim their nose and ear hair. Nor use an ancient microwave-sterilizer that probably irradiated combs sooner than it cleaned them. His legacy is now some namby-pamby Paul's Boutique, with a lusty interior design that once spurred a mate of mine to knock on the window and ask 'Is this a brothel?' The police were called.

There is a stigma attached to staying somewhere long enough to see change. The place has to be worth it, and most people question whether Barton is. I dug up a video showing the Barton of 1987; it pans around our town centre with 'Dreaming' by Orchestral Manoeuvres as the soundtrack. There's so much space back then. It shows inside the pubs that are now in disrepair, and the lights do that weird trailing thing on the old fashioned film. It jumps inside a car, driving up Ferriby Road, past my Grand-father's house, into the nothingness that's now the two-hundred house estate I live in.

My Grandfather, ninety years old, has barely been able to move from the seat by his front window for a decade. It overlooks one hundred meters of Ferriby Road. And he just watches it. Once a year, the Humber Bridge marathon jogs past. Once a year, there may be snow. A couple of times a day, an ambulance will scream by. Once a day, the postwoman wheels down the drive. The grand clock in the hallway chimes out the hour. Each individual day stretches out like a lethargic eternity; yet when he looks back, the waiting time between each snowfall, siren, visitor, is so redundant that it didn't happen. The memorable events collapse together. Time speeds up. The leaves on the front garden's tree grow and fall, grow and fall. The long nights pull in and retreat again and again, like the world is blinking.

The sun's not up yet. I'm seventeen, and I cross the road where I should've caught the bus, hopping a fence into Top Field.

I turn to watch the bus pass that gap in the trees, and feel safe and terrified. My cheeks are whipped by the wind; the field sucks on my footsteps and smells of wet leaf and dog shit. At yon end is a spine of old trees with paths hidden in it. I slump down, careful of those frozen roots and low branches. Here's where we used to do Turbos, where you breathe in and out as hard as you can, and then stand straight and everyone pushes you by the chest against that tree until you pass out. Once, Tit wouldn't wake up and we got scared, and when he did his eyes were a bit yellow; once, James said 'make sure you see me - see me - watch me - don't let me hit my head' whilst unconscious; once, I apparently had a little fit.

This tree got burnt down. People have fires in that pit there, and get pissed. But when it was alive, people used to nail rope-swings on to it. We were climbing it once, and way up on that horizontal branch Shaun's sovereign ring got caught perfectly in a hammered-flat old nail, and he was hung off it by the finger when his grip lost out.

And here's Tree Field. A big, unused park, on our outskirts. I was here, helping to plant saplings in the naked mud when I was four. A woman gave me a spade and asked if I'd been eating my Weetabix. It's tall and thick now, with bushes and long grass and a gazillion spiders between each trunk. I've passed these two dog walkers every morning for months now; they always say hello, but must wonder what I'm doing here at half seven every morning. The sun starts to show through the twiggy canopy and red berries. I've kept track of the days getting shorter. How far I am from home when I first see the sun. How many leaves are left on the trees. The colours. The first morning frosts appearing then thickening. I think about my Granddad. I made a little mark on one of the trees in September and now it's nearly healed. Here yesterday, I'll be here tomorrow.

I make it to a plain field beyond and look up the spot where me and Matt were rolling those cigarettes after the Dead Semester gig. To Death Hill, on my right from down here. There's machinery blowing a gale now. Reflector coats walk about rubbing their hands, digging holes and laying concrete. Since coming here, I've watched the show home go up, and I'm scared I'll see the whole place finished before I'm cured.

Four years on, I'm not glued here anymore, but I still feel the stigma every time I notice something new. Will there be another video I'll find in twenty five years: Barton 2012, before we seeped into Barrow, New Holland, South Ferriby, Horkstow and Barrow Haven? Before a second comprehensive school had to be opened? Before our first six-storey building? Before St. Peter's got knocked down? Before our first night club? Before Tesco got shunned by Waitrose?

Will I have seen it happen firsthand?

Barton was once in South Humberside. Now we're in North Lincolnshire. We kind of got repositioned in the nineties. Away from association with the Humber, perhaps. Barton was turned around and told to face South, told to move on. Go in the naughty corner. We are not defined by being South of Hull anymore, apparently, we're now North of Lincoln. And then the bridge toll continued to rise, as though Hull wanted to cut all ties with us. What if Lincoln decides they don't want us anymore? We'll eventually be classed as East Belfast or West Hamburg! Barton shouldn't be defined parasitically, a place near to bigger places. We're large and infamous enough to be our own town now. I might hope to grow up and grow out of it, but Barton's growing too. Maybe everyone who's too good for it will one day have kids in London who can't wait to finish Uni and go to work in Barton, the capital city.

Or one might say 'Come on kids, let me show you Hull, where I used to study.'

'Where's Hull?'

'You know, that little place in North Bartonshire.'

Writing *Hull*

The Tattooed Earl

Lorraine Gouland

It's a dark and drizzly evening and I'm in Hull for a Merchant Navy medical. It's a long drive from where I live. Two hours cooped up in the car with my boyfriend, both of us trying to navigate through the rain-spotted windscreen. I don't know about the rest of the city, but the bit we're in appears to have been designed for those who are going somewhere – somewhere else. Flyovers, dual carriageways, arterial roads choked with queues of traffic lead us around in circles until, finally, we spot a hotel.

February is a gloomy month in any part of England. For a West Country flower like me, uprooted and replanted in Yorkshire, the North East is especially cold and glum but after booking a room and before dinner, we decide to get out and stretch our legs.

Ambling along accompanied by the rumble and swish of tyres on the wet road beside us, we pass buildings, bushes and bus parks. Then, there's a three-storey black-and-white structure with a green ornamental arch peeping over the shuttering ply that shrouds its first floor.

I stop and look up. Above me, swinging free and squeaky in the wintry bluster is a pub sign. I squint at it. A very bearded Victorian type squints back at me. Below him are the words Free House. Above him it says The Earl De Grey.

Hull tilts and slides away. Rain-dirty pavements become a painted steel deck that moves under my feet …

It's 1984. I'm a nineteen-year-old deckhand on an oil rig standby vessel 100 miles north-east of the Shetland Islands. Over the ship's port side, a collection of girders and portacabins balances on three enormous, rusty legs. The agitated, gunmetal-grey sea rises and slaps the legs with foamy hands. This is what we've come all the way from Lowestoft to stand by: the Brent Bravo, a platform built to harvest the oil and gas from beneath the North Sea.

The other platforms of the Brent Field stand between us and the horizon: the Alpha, the Charlie, the Delta and the Spar. Look carefully and somewhere below each is an antique Hull trawler wallowing in the swell. We are the cavalry. If there's an accident – a fire, a fall, a downed helicopter - we will charge to the rescue, black smoke belching from our funnels. We are primed, trained, ready. And really, really bored.

Geoff's curly black hair is being raked by the wind into wild wiry spikes that stand vertically from his head. His yellow plastic trousers stretch over his pot belly as he bends and drags his brush back and forth across the deck. Moving over to him, I point to the faded blue letters looping across his forearm.

'Why does that say Duke of Earl?'

He looks at me, his face puckered into an angry sneer. 'Fuck off, you nosy bastard,' he says and stomps away to scrub somewhere else.

'Fine.' I pull a face at his retreating back, and dip my brush into the bucket of soapy water. The wind whips the suds from the top, splattering them against my legs. Scrubbing the decks is a once-a-trip treat to stop us fomenting mutiny in our boredom. The sound of bristles against steel sets my teeth on edge so I sing out loud to mask it.

'Duke/Duke/Duke/Duke of Earl/Duke/Duke/Duke of Earl ...'

'Will you give over singing that stupid song?' The cook, Charlie, is halfway through a thin, prison-style roll-up cigarette. Convicts and sailors all smoke skinny fags, makes the tobacco stretch further.

'I can't, it's stuck in my head.' I'm bending over the cardboard box that contains the ship's library, looking for one book, just one, which I haven't read. 'Anyway, it's Geoff's fault. I didn't know he was a Darts fan.'

'Darts? What the fuck are you on about, you daft bint?' It's the end of the day; Charlie and I are in the mess – a room with two long tables separated by benches. This is our lounge – no carpets, no cushions, just hard wooden seats and chipped paint.

'Duke of Earl. The song, by Darts. He's got it on his arm.' I feel safe to mention the tattoo. Geoff is tucked away in his cabin with a stash of porn magazines.

A slender twist of smoke rises from the stub between Charlie's nicotine-brown fingers to join the blue haze hanging below the strip lights. The smoke zigzags. Charlie's still got the shakes from his last time home. He comes to sea to dry out.

He laughs and inhales on his cigarette. Smoke gusts from his mouth. He coughs, wipes tears from his eyes and laughs again.

'Duke of Earl! Fucking hell!'

At the other table, Paul and Frank, two engineers, still wearing their grimy overalls, pause in their cribbage match to eavesdrop on the conversation.

Charlie drops his roll-up into the corned-beef can that serves as an ashtray.

'It's supposed to say Earl De Grey.'

'Earl de Grey...?' I'm mystified.

Paul lays aside his cards and glares up at me from under the unkempt grey garden of his eyebrows. Not for the first time I wonder if he lets them grow to compensate for the lack of hair on his head.

'Fucking split-arse,' he taunts. 'Can tell you're not from 'Ull.'

He's right, I'm not and neither is Charlie. Along with the Captain and the Chief Engineer, Charlie's from Grimsby. He's a Grimmy, a Yella Belly. The rest of the crew are from Hull. All eight of them. The Grimmies and I are outnumbered. If you're from Hull, you're a Hully-Gully, a Yorkie, and you don't like anyone who isn't from Hull – especially if they're from Grimsby. Since the first coracles set out to go fishing, the rivalry between the two ports has festered. Even now, at the end of the twentieth century, with the fishing industry breathing its last, that rivalry's as bitter as ever. Yorkies claim to have the moral advantage as, according to them, 'God were born in 'Ull.' Apparently, 'it took God six days to make 'Ull and on the seventh, he put all the shit round it.' Grimmies respond by saying the Humber Bridge is the road from nowhere to nothing. None of these men are fishing now. Economics have driven them, en masse, onto standby boats but still, Grimmies hate Yorkies and Yorkies hate Grimmies.

Except Charlie. No one hates Charlie. Besides, you don't mess with the cook. He's the one person aboard who could, if he was of a mind to, exact a terrible revenge whenever he felt like it.

'I'll give you Yorkie bastards one thing.' Charlie raises an eyebrow in the direction of the engineers. 'The Earl De Grey is a pretty good pub.'

'Listen to that cheeky cunt, Paul.' Frank nudges his mate. Angry patches flare on his cheeks, competing with his bulbous boozer's nose for redness. 'Pretty fucking good? That pub's world famous. You get sailors from all over in there. India, China, you name it. The first thing they do when their ships dock is ask the way to the Earl De Grey.'

'Oh I know,' Charlie answers. 'But that's cos it's a right fucking bag shop.'

'A bag shop?' I've lost interest in the book box now.

'Yeah, you know, if you want to get yourself an old bag.' Charlie flicks a clump of his greasy brown hair out of his eyes.

'He means a whore.' Paul is busy rolling a fag. Shreds of tobacco fall across the table top. He blows them away before continuing. 'There's some very accommodating ladies in the Earl De Grey.'

'Ah.' The conversation is heading into hazardous waters for me. I wait for the men to round on me, asking why I'm at sea when I'm literally sitting on my fortune. If they were women, I've been told, they'd be at home 'selling their holes'. I hold my breath, waiting, but then Charlie smirks.

'Shows you what kind of women they've got in 'Ull.'

Frank isn't known for his sense of humour.

'Listen, them lasses are from Grimsby. They had to come up to 'Ull to go with fishermen what earned real money.'

'Hold on, hold on,' I break in, relieved not to be the subject of the banter. 'Why does Geoff's tattoo say Duke of Earl, though?'

The men laugh long and loud. I wait until their chuckles give way to splutters and ask again.

'C'mon, why does it say Duke of Earl?'

Paul rubs a grease-ingrained hand across the top of his bald head. Over the noise of the ship's generators thrumming away beneath my feet, I can hear the scratch of his rough palm sand-papering his scalp.

'You know what a cocky twat Geoff is?' he asks the room in general. We all nod.

'Well, he were always like that – even when he were a teenager. He got that tattoo when he were seventeen. Just docked from his first trip away on a trawler. Been fishing up in Icelandic waters and he thought he were John Wayne. So the lads took him up the Earl de Grey. Said they were going to make a man of him.'

'They did that all right,' Frank butts in. 'What were the name of that tart they set him up with?'

'Stella.' Paul frowns at him, frustrated at the interruption.

'Stella!' Frank ignores the frown. 'Fuck, she were an ugly cow.'

'Are you going to shut up?' Paul rounds on him. 'I'm trying to tell the lass a yarn!' Paul picks up the thread of his story again. 'Anyway, Stella took young Geoff round the back of the pub and introduced him to some earthly delights.' He squashes out his roll-up between his fingers and drops it in the ashtray.

'He were grinning like an idiot when he come back in.'

'Is that it?' I'm trying to laugh quietly behind my hand. 'It's a memorial to the night he lost his cherry?'

'Yeah, well ...' Paul reaches for his tobacco tin. 'After that he kept drinking till he fell over. And he threw up on me shoes, the cunt. Hundred quid, them shoes cost me. I had to throw them away.' He falls quiet, staring off down memory lane. It seems he's still mourning his lost footwear.

Frank steps into the sudden silence. 'He were still pissed up next dinner time. Showed us this fucking tattoo he'd had done. Weren't till we took him outside and showed him the pub sign that he realised his mistake.'

'Be fair.' Charlie leans forward on his bench. 'The pub did change its name –'

'In 1872!' Frank snaps back. 'We're talking about 1974 here. And even then it were called the Junction Dock Tavern not the Duke of fucking Earl!'

'Oh aye, you just had to tell her, didn't you?' A voice from the doorway makes us all jump. 'You gobby bastards.' Geoff glares at Paul and Frank. 'Bet they never told you about the parrots, did they?' he asks me. I shake my head.

'No, thought not.' He tucks the bundle of magazines he's carrying under his arm and leans against the door. 'There's two parrots in that pub, Cha Cha and Ringo. Right chatty bastards they are. I caught these two bollock-brains teaching them to say "Show us your tattoo, Geoff, show us your tattoo."'

'Did it work?'

'No, thank fuck.'

'Should've taught them that song of yours.' Charlie sniggers. 'How does it go, lass?'

'Duke/Duke/Duke/Duke of Earl,' I start.

Then the lads join in. 'Duke/Duke/Duke of Earl.'

'Ah, get fucked, all of you.' Geoff strides off down the alleyway and out of sight.

180 years. That's how long Hull's most infamous pub traded for. And

I missed it. I heard all about it but I never clapped eyes on it, until now.

Shockingly cold rain spatters my upturned face as I peer at the creaking sign.

'What're you looking at?'

'This is the Earl De Grey.' I wave my free hand towards the dark, boarded-up and silent pub.

'Ri-ight. And is that supposed to mean something to me?'

I lower my eyes from the bearded visage of the original Earl De Grey, Lord High Steward of Hull and study my bloke. I must be looking at the only Yorkshire sailor who's never heard of this pub.

'It was very famous in its day.' I start to laugh. 'I used to sail with this cook, Charlie. He told me he met a woman in there once who reckoned she could pee higher up the wall than him. And she did.'

'Wow. Sounds like quite a pub. Did you ever go in there?'

'No.'

'Glad to hear it.' He puts his arm around me and we turn back the way we've come. The rain's getting heavier but with our backs to the wind, the walk is easier. I do look back though. Just once.

'They used to have a couple of parrots in there, you know?'

'Yeah? Did they talk?'

'Yes, but Charlie said that burglars murdered one of them in 1985.'

'Murdered? Why would anyone murder a parrot?'

'Maybe they thought it would grass on them.'

'What about the other one?'

'It never spoke again.'

'So the burglars silenced both of them.'

'Yeah ...' I pull him forward. 'Let's go eat.'

Halfway back to the hotel, I realise that I'm humming. I nudge my boyfriend with my elbow and take a deep breath.

'Duke/Duke/Duke/Duke of Earl.'

Writing *Hull*

Spurn Point, September 2010

Matthew Shaw

This sight is incredible. As we stand on this bunker of sand and long, dry grass, the sea comes in at us from both sides. To the right, there's the freezing North Sea and, to the other, the widening Humber Estuary flowing into that same, vast, body of water.

We're joined by a strong wind today. The migrating birds, especially the smaller species, are struggling against it as they fly out to sea: beginning their crazy-sounding journeys to warmer weather. I understand the desire to leave our typical, British freezing forecasts behind. But if I were that tiny, that vulnerable, I'd think again. Maybe tucking myself away in some bush or tree would be preferable to getting lost at sea.

Here we are, then, my mother and me: getting away from the city and our city-based lives for a few hours. I've only ever been here once before, back when I was eleven years old. That was at the height of my bird-watching phase. I'd say it lasted, in a serious way, for a few more years, but I've never really stopped being interested in it – to some degree – and in the last couple of years that interest has begun to bloom again. And Spurn Point is a wonderful, rich place to visit.

I suppose there are also other motives for us being here – other, more far-reaching, close-to-philosophical reasons. Perhaps that's a rather grand way of describing things that are, to us at least, routine and ordinary, but standing here on this sandbank, that's a bit like how it feels.

Since my father had a serious stroke nearly three years ago, we've taken every opportunity to get out to do and see things. Thankfully we have many similar interests, so going to places like this or out to the cinema or to a comedy gig are rarely a tug-of-war match over who gets to make the final decision. And I suppose, essentially, without wishing to make this sound too soppy, it's good to just spend time together, to share a few memories while we're both at an age where we can understand and appreciate them. The suddenness with which Dad's illness came should teach us that at least.

I vaguely remember the immediate days, in the hospital, by his bed. I'd just started my second year at university, got about two weeks in, when it happened.

I never knew what a stroke was before then, never given it any real attention. For some reason, I used to think it was to do with the heart, because I'd always associated it with a heart attack, and perhaps also because the name 'stroke' reminds me, weirdly, of a heartbeat. Thinking about it now, I can't explain why that is: that association was just always in my head, the first thing that popped up whenever it appeared in a TV medical drama or I heard about one in the news. I think I should have paid more attention to those media references; maybe if I had I'd have got the actual, full picture: at the very least, realised which part of the body it affected.

That aside, though, the actuality and realness of a stroke is something I do now know. It came to me instantly. Dad was in bed for weeks, in a kind of hazy paralysis: hardly able to move, completely disabled down the left side, his brain utterly shot by the huge haemorrhage he'd suffered. It's difficult to tell what was happening inside his head at that time. He'd go through all kinds of hallucinations – like believing his shoulder was made out of metal – and when he looked at you it was like he couldn't compute what was coming in through his eyes because of the immense brain damage. Most of the time he didn't speak any real sense.

And nowadays, I suppose it's half-and-half as to whether he speaks sense – or, more accurately, 60:40 (with nonsense winning the larger chunk). And Mum might argue the proportion of rubbish is greater – she's exposed to more of it.

The other day I told him he was going to have to put his teeth in – he has dentures for the top of his mouth. When I got them ready and put them down in front of him, he looked a little flustered.

'I haven't got me other ones out,' he stuttered.

When I questioned him – because now I was getting confused – he thought he had a second pair of teeth and that he was still wearing them. I've no idea how he decided that, why he'd need a second, spare set – and I'd guess that he didn't either. I suppose he can't really think things through anymore.

We have this theory in our house: that a lot of what Dad says when asked about something is just the first thing that occurs to him. And often the answer is 'Yes' no matter what the enquiry, even if it's a two (or more) part question.

'Do you want some cheesecake or angel delight for pudding?'

'Yes.'

We've had a peaceful morning out here. But the birds have been a little difficult. They're loads of wading birds and ducks and gulls out by the low tide, but it is a very low tide and my basic binoculars struggle to pull them into focus and clarity.

The faux expertise I displayed on the car journey here has been utterly wasted. I flicked through my bird book, asserting that we'd probably see that, and that one too, but now we're here I can't quite join the image with what sits somewhere out by the water and make a positive, certain identification.

I so admire those that can. By one line of white feathers they're able to say what something is – and even whether it's a juvenile or some sort of vagrant, mixed-bred version. They have different eyes than I do. Obviously, biologically speaking they do, but they look at things in such a way, a way I've not mastered yet, instantly setting upon the tiny distinctions that separate one from another – and they do so without a flash of doubt.

I don't mind, though. It's been a long time since the whole reason for coming to places like this was about seeing as many different species as possible, while, ideally, adding a bunch of new ones to the list of birds that I have seen. It always used to be important to me, that: every time I was in a sort of nature hot spot, I really wanted to see something I never had before. And I had a childish sureness about it that surpassed sense. It was the kind of certainty that wholeheartedly believed that the sparrow or dunnock I'd just seen was in fact some kind of rare warbler or finch. As a child, I would scan my bird book so voraciously that my eyes would see whatever I wanted them to, whether it was realistic or not. I'd ignore the little maps that reliably informed the reader that you were only ever likely to see that bird on the Mediterranean coast of Europe and North Africa; instead, I'd assume that that was what just flew by me and briefly sat on the branch opposite... in a field in Norfolk.

But, despite our basic contentment at just being out here, we do end up seeing a few interesting things – though, now I will always be tentative about new sightings, slow to confirm, repeatedly checking and counter-checking with the book. Does it have those markings on the wings? Does it say this is their sort of habitat? I no longer trust whatever instinct I had as a young bird-watcher.

The whole time we've been here, there have been little groups, about half-a-dozen or a dozen in number, of small, strong-voiced meadow pipits passing through. Before we came out here I consulted the website of the Bird Observatory that keeps a record of those that make Spurn Point a part of their migration journey. I don't ever recall seeing them before and small, brown birds, especially while they're flying, still all look the same to me, so I wanted to know beforehand what we would have a good chance of being joined by out here. As they fly in an up-and-down, almost faltering way (that is only in part a result of the strong, coastal winds) they sing too. And they only stop singing once they've landed somewhere. They're in for a long flight and their song-voice will have to last the distance like the little wings they've got to rely on.

This positive identification is, if I'm honest, a slightly retrospective one. Although I expect to see many of them out here – at this time of year, hundreds fly through most days – as they flit above our heads, calling away, all I am certain about is that I've never encountered them before. At first, I wonder if they're a finch or a bunting or whether they could belong to the warbler family. But then, driving away from the peninsula, I glance to the left of the road and see one of them stood on the putting green of a golf course: its shape and gait practically identical to the drawings I'm used to referring to. (After a few more days, I looked to see if the website had been updated to include the information for the day we visited. They counted 339 meadow pipits that day – enough confirmation for me).

These sorts of days are vital for Mum – chances to be out of a house that holds so much responsibility and few moments where she can be 'off duty'. Maybe we're luckier than others who are in similar situations – we do get two respite days a week, 9 till 5. But Dad's needs are pretty intense, and on a monthly basis almost, they seem to be getting greater. I think it's been over a year now since he's been able to stand with any real strength in his one good leg – and even when he could, that was with help from at least one other person.

We have about another hour, roughly, and decide to wander down the slim, sand-covered road, back in the direction we drove in from. The tide is less expansive this way and there are reed beds and movement – perhaps a better chance to see stuff.

Along the way, down on the mudflats, is a lone redshank pecking away in the little pools the rocks and sand have helped to form. It's so close, a hundred yards maybe, that I almost don't need any extra help to see the giveaway characteristic – long, red legs. I use my binoculars anyway, just so I'm sure.

Further along, in among the reed beds, are a few large, all-white bodies moving about. Initially I file them away as swans. That guess comes from nothing more than seeing their white shapes briefly, in the distance, and as we get closer we see they're walking upright, heron-like. I realise therefore that they must be little egrets, slightly shorter than the common, grey heron, with black legs and yellow toes and a long, straight black bill. Another first. As we continue to walk towards them and the reed beds, more appear and by the time we're heading back to the car, we've seen around half-a-dozen.

As we drive back over where we've just walked, past the reed beds and the egrets, we're a little ahead of ourselves. We don't need to be back on the main road, heading to Hull, just yet. There's a little building, a kind of whitewashed cottage that at the same time as looking like it could be a kind of visitors centre, looks nowhere near warm enough to be habitable.

We park up nearby, alongside some other cars, and walk round the back to look out at the North Sea coast. There's a small, wooden hide – one that's typical in design to what you'd see at any other birding place. Alongside that, backs to the sea, are two men sat in foldaway camping chairs. I'm about to walk round the back of the hide, to the door, when I notice why the two men are sat facing away from the beach and the birds behind them.

It's because they have their own bird that they're watching.

In the grass it sits, still and calm. I don't know what it is exactly, at first, except that it's a bird of prey. So as not to disturb it, we walk round the front of the hide – instead disturbing the people that have their lenses fixed to the coastline. After a little deliberation – do I want to embarrass myself, show that I have no idea what I'm looking at, even though it's a few feet away from me, not moving a muscle, an identification-dream? – I muster the courage to speak, quietly:

'What's wrong with it?'

'It got caught out by a crow. Tried attacking it down by the sea there and ended up getting wet. We've dried it off and ringed it. Now we're just waiting to see that it flies off safely.'

'Right. And what is it?'

'A juvenile peregrine.'

Those things are the scourge of pigeons and other smaller, city birds, but here it is staring right back at us, no threat. For a minute I wonder whether it will actually fly away, whether its instincts have been washed out of it. That's a silly thought, though, to accompany a bizarre story: nature will win out here. Without human help, it may not have got out of the water, that can be hypothesised, but now it sits, dry and rested, nothing will keep it from riding the winds again. It simply has to do it, and we walk away from it with a similar conviction: the time we set aside has gone, washed over and through us like the sea might over a young, misguided peregrine.

Writing *Hull*

Hilary versus Hitler

David Tomlinson

During 1941, when viewed from the top of the Yorkshire Wolds, the eastern skyline often pulsed like a livid red scar. But it was not the inspirational light of a rising sun. It was a burning city, the most bombed place in Britain after London.

It was Hull.

The long established and well equipped port, close to mainland Europe, was a prime target. Much of the city centre was razed to the ground during the bombardments. 1,185 people were killed, a fifth of whom were children. Ninety-five per cent of the city's houses were damaged or destroyed, and out of a population of 320,000, 192,000 were made homeless.

One of those fleeing the northern blitz to the refuge of the Wolds was eight-year-old Hilary Walker, along with her twin sister, Betty, and their mother, Evelyn.

Hilary was born in Anlaby, Hull, at 12.15am on 4th December 1931, a year after Hitler and his National Socialist Workers Party had won 107 seats in the German Parliament, and a year before it became the largest party in the country. Hilary was blissfully unaware of Hitler's progress, and the rest of the world was largely unconcerned by it.

Hilary's arrival at Anlaby was something of a surprise; an hour earlier Betty had been born. Nobody realised Betty was a twin at this point. It was before the days of pre-natal scanning. During the latter stages of her pregnancy, Evelyn had only been able to walk by holding onto the backs of chairs. Her bump was so huge, she half-expected the baby to walk out of its own accord. The fact that Betty weighed less than five pounds was Evelyn's first shock. The second, and by far the bigger of the two, was the gradual appearance of another baby's head sixty minutes later. The midwife had to chase the doctor down the street shouting, 'Wait, there's one more!" At least, Evelyn hoped it was only one more.

The girls grew up sharing a bedroom in the suburbs of Hull and Hilary has happy childhood memories of identical favourite toys. "We had two of everything to make it fair. Our room was like a Noah's Ark of playthings. We did have to share the best toy of all, though – a pedal car with an ice-cream label."

The sisters earned their pocket money of 6d (later raised to 8d) by helping with the housework. "On wash days the house filled with steam from the copper boiler, and putting clothes through the mangles was hard labour. But it was worth it for the sweets. We spent our money on aniseed balls and Cadbury's chocolate."

Hilary's schooling started at Eastfield Road Council School at the age of five, shortly after Hitler announced, in defiance of the Treaty of Versailles, that he intended to rearm Germany. While Hitler continued to rail against the punitive terms of the treaty and the recent history of his country, Hilary moved onto to Kirk Ella church school. She remembers the Sunday treat of going to Megginson's tea-shop at Nafferton with its red and white Gingham table cloths. "We used to go on a Sunday afternoon. They did the most marvellous toast and jam…and cakes, of course."

Hitler's idea of fun, on the other hand, was to order troops into the 'demilitarised' zone of the Rhineland. Britain made no attempt to resist him at this point – too fearful perhaps of jeopardising Sunday tea at Megginson's. For the time being the English way of life continued with blinkered optimism and Hilary's regular treats remained uninterrupted. Riley's ice-cream delivered in tubs on Saturdays; day trips to Hornsea beach; holidays at Bridlington and Filey; and visits to Goathland where her Aunty Doris lived in the 'fresh air' recuperating from tuberculosis. Hitler also stayed busy. He seized Austria, announcing Anschluss (union with Germany) in 1938, and in the autumn of the same year went on to seize a part of

Czechoslovakia.

Hilary's holidays to Brid and Filey were an important part of her youth. She has photos of beach chalets on wheels and recalls the beach tents being erected. "The man used to arrive to put the tent up. You chose your pitch and then he would come along with this canvas, with this floor, and then he'd put the canvas bit on."

While hiring a beach chalet was more ambitious than hiring a deckchair it was not quite as ambitious as camping out in the Slav lands and absorbing what remained of Czechoslovakia. The principle was the same, though. Hitler chose his pitch (in someone else's country) and then his troops set up camp.

Hilary's memory of these dramatic events is locked into her childhood perspective and consequently comes out in a childlike voice. "There were these huge rumours going round that we were definitely thinking of going to war. In his wisdom Chamberlain decided he would go and see old Adolf Hitler. He came back saying 'peace for our time' but the bit of paper he had it written on was absolutely useless."

At eight years old Hilary's perception of the international drama may not have embraced all the political subtleties involved but she knew something serious was happening from the reactions of her parents. "Nobody was allowed to talk when the news came on the radio. It had to be absolute hush. Mum and Dad would sit up close to the speaker and look at each other. There was something in the silence and their faces…We knew things weren't right, that something was hanging, waiting to happen."

Germany invaded Poland in the early morning hours of September 1st 1939. On September 3rd at 11.15am, Chamberlain addressed the nation over the radio and declared the country was now at war. "It is the evil things we shall be fighting against – brute force, bad faith, injustice, oppression, and persecution – and against them I am certain that the right will prevail."

And so Hilary and her sister were evacuated to the Wolds, accompanied by their mum. Hilary's father, Norman, owned a tool hire company and therefore his contribution to the fight kept him in Hull, maintaining and repairing essential machinery on the docks and helping to make stricken ships seaworthy again.

According to Hilary, "the Wolds swarmed with evacuated children", and finding accommodation for them was not easy. "The children were subject to the luck of the draw when it came to their new homes. People took them in…farmers…but there was no room, really, you see."

Hilary was one of the fortunate ones. She was a private evacuee. Her mother could afford to rent a property, which meant they didn't have to rely on local charity like most of the other children. "They used to get off their buses or trains and were then lined up. They all had labels on their coats, pinned on their jackets to tell you what their names were. Whoever had come to offer board and lodge would eye them up and say, 'I'll have that one'. And then sometimes they wouldn't take brothers and sisters into the same house. They probably preferred to have two girls and so the brothers and sisters were split up, which was absolutely traumatic." The plight of these uprooted children arouses strong memories in Hilary. She has grandchildren and the thought of them lining up with labels around their necks gives her the shivers. "They were horrible – some of the families to these children. Really horrible. But fortunately it wasn't the case for all of them. Some of them had a really good time. Like I say, it was luck of the draw."

But evacuees were not the only new inhabitants on the Wolds; a large proportion of the failed British Expeditionary force was also billeted there. The Wolds provided the necessary space to camp and train. "The war was escalating. The soldiers came back from Dunkirk. They had to re-group and get the army sorted out. I know there were a lot of tanks and things about. They were everywhere. The troops lived under canvas – in the fields, woods, you name it. That's why there aren't many hedges on the Wolds. They were levelled so that tanks and heavy artillery could move about more freely."

Amongst the many uniforms, Hilary was surprised to occasionally hear a foreign accent. The Wolds, she discovered, had also become the home of the Free French. General De Gaulle had made an appeal on BBC Radio, June 18th 1940, which was recognised as the official start of the French Resistance movement. In 1942 he sent a handful of men and women back into occupied France to work undercover. The resistance became known as the Maquis, and the heroism of its members is legendary. Hilary is proud to think she spent time as a neighbour of some of this elite group.

Although Hilary never met de Gaulle, her father did. "A French ship had limped into port, badly damaged after an air attack. My father and his crew worked day and night to repair it, and so de Gaulle came down to thank them all. They all had to stand in a line and shake hands with him, and when he got to my father he said, 'I thank you for a wonderful ship it is better than you.' He meant to say 'better than new'. He could speak English but it sounded like 'better than you.' And that caused a bit of merriment, I think. Of course, the shoe was on the other foot after the war when we went on holiday to France and my dad couldn't even say 'bonjour' without making the French laugh at his dreadful accent."

The twins fared much better with their French and Hilary's sister Betty ended up working in Paris. Their education on the Wolds began at Lund Primary School. "There were only two teachers: Miss Ireland and Mrs Carter, the Head Mistress. Ah, she was a disciplinarian but my goodness she was a good teacher. Miss Ireland was very kind and very gentle. We had to walk three miles to the school from the farm and then three miles back and so we couldn't go home at lunchtime because there wasn't time. Miss Ireland would always make Bett and I a marvellous, steaming hot cup of cocoa…I can still taste it."

A cup of hot cocoa on a cold day was often all it took to keep the war at bay for a moment. Despite the uncertainty of what lay ahead, the British population made every effort to keep everything business as usual. "We just lived a normal sort of life, really. It's difficult to describe in a way. We rarely felt threatened…that we had to be careful, or anything…" It took the sound of sirens to bring the fear of war close to home. "The Air Raid Warden's post was opposite the Chapel, so we did have a warning when danger was imminent. When the sirens went they sent us out of school. We had to get home. And I used to think that was so funny. We were quite scared actually when we came out of school. We used to run so fast to get home in case anything happened. And that was supposed to be a safe thing to do. We often wondered afterwards whether it was. But I suppose it was just a question of getting back to your loved ones, really."

No matter what Hilary felt, the Wolds were not as safe as was first supposed. After the German planes had finished their raids on Hull they would drop any surplus bombs on their return flight. "It was very bad at times. I sometimes saw the planes caught in the searchlights as they headed back after a raid. And if they had any bombs left they just used to let them go wherever…it didn't matter where it was. It happened a few times. This bungalow we lived in had this kind of dado rail at the top. There were all these plates sitting on the top. Nobody ever thought to screw them to the wall. Every time there was a bomb nearby the house shook and the plates fell to the floor and smashed. I've got a photograph somewhere where one of the high headquarters officers came to have a look at one of the craters, and he's actually standing in the crater and inspecting it. I don't know what he hoped to find."

While Hilary couldn't hear the bombing raids on Hull, she could often see the horrific consequences from the heights of the Wolds. "You could see the glow from the top of the Wolds. I think that was the worst. And we worried about Dad and Gran. Gran was bombed out. That was right at the end of the war. There was one dropped behind her house. My aunty and her were sitting around the fire. They were drying some clothes on a clothes horse in front of the fire and the blast, it knocked all the windows out, and they were still sitting there. I think they were fairly shocked but they weren't injured. But from that day to this they've never discovered where those clothes went to. They just disappeared. I think they were probably sucked up the chimney. When I think about it now I get an image of a Luftwaffe pilot suddenly being presented with a pair of Granny's bloomers across his cockpit window and returning to Germany dressed like Widow Twankey."

This is how, without realising it, Hilary did her fighting during the war. She joked a lot. The whole country did. And the more extreme Hitler's behaviour, the more the nation poked fun at him. Belittling Hitler through humour is not a retrospective phenomenon, it's how his enemies dealt with him at the time. Hilary's humour was forged during a period when it was needed the most; the blacker the future looked, the sillier the humour became. "The radio was everything during the war; the fastest source of information and the greatest source of entertainment." The mood of the country oscillated on its airwaves. One place on the dial brought something as serious as the declaration of war, another brought Tommy Handley. "There were lovely programmes like ITMA (It's That Man Again) and they were funny. They were really funny. Workers Playtime, was that Arthur Askey? Flanagan and Allen and the Crazy Gang. Then there was George Formby and his Ukulele. It was all so simple when you think about it today. But it was really funny. And it was necessary. The Windmill Theatre stayed open all the time. It got bombed but it still kept on going. And you still had your cinema."

Radio was intimate, but theatre and cinema were communal. Laughter around the radio uplifted, but laughter in the aisles fortified. The country was in this thing together and nowhere amplified that as much as an audience in front of a stage or a silver screen. "On our birthdays our mother always gave us a treat in the form of

Mr Parsons and his 'complete cinematograph show.'"

But no amount of distractions could keep the war permanently at bay and not every explosion was a near miss. The injuries ranged from the comic to the tragic. During one raid the Commanding Officer suffered a bruised knee when he tripped over the vicar's bicycle left outside a house he was visiting. On another occasion Brigadier DW Furlong was, with a young Lieutenant billeted in the village, inspecting a minefield laid near the coast in case of invasion. One of the mines blew up and killed both men. A large military funeral was held in the village and the Lieutenant was buried in the local cemetery. "It was quiet. Like all the grown-ups had taken a day off from coping and putting on a brave face. It was the first time I'd seen a coffin – shiny handles on it, and I thought that's not right. Nothing should be shining today. It shouldn't be sunny."

The sun, however, was to be the backdrop of some of the bloodiest scenes when shortly after the evacuation of Dunkirk the fighting transferred significantly from the beaches to the skies. From August 13th to September 17th 1940 the Battle of Britain blazed above the English coast and over the Channel. A small group of extraordinary men stalled the German war machine and defeated Goering's effort to establish air superiority, inspiring Churchill to say, "Never in the field of human conflict was so much owed by so many to so few." Hitler was forced to postpone his invasion of England and the country's collective sigh of relief appeared to manifest itself in songs. "People were singing songs everywhere, some of them I don't suppose I was meant to hear – too rude for a young girl, but I always smile when I watch Dad's Army and listen to Bud Flanagan sing that line 'Who do you think you are kidding Mr Hitler, if you think old England's done.' It wasn't, you see. We weren't. The people."

Hilary was amongst the lucky ones. Her family survived the war intact, and so did Megginson's Tea Room. Britain celebrated Hitler's defeat on VE day, but for Hilary it was marked by a more tangible event. At the outbreak of hostilities her father and some workmates had been responsible for transferring a statue of King William III from the docks (where it stood) to the safety of a farm in the countryside. "Where he was then buried in a haystack. King Billy, not my dad." Hilary's humour also survived the war intact. "It was a matter of pride for the council, you see. They didn't want the Germans to get hold of King Billy. After the war when they took him back to be returned to his plinth, Dad took us with him. It was quite symbolic, returning the king to his throne. And that's when I really knew that Hitler was gone forever."

Hilary – now eighty years old – revisits her refugee view from the top of the Wolds and considers the 'evil things' that she as a child had to fight against, and the evil things that remain so prevalent in so many parts of the world. "I outlived Hitler but not war." She adjusts her weight on her two walking sticks and takes a long look at the east coast skyline through blue-framed glasses. The view is grey and be-speckled with fine rain but Hilary's eyes still reflect a blaze. "'Peace for our time'? It was ridiculous," she says, "Nothing's changed, has it, really?"

Writing *Hull*

Madame Clapham: a history of Hull couture

Maria Stead

Peeking through the letterbox, thousands of pins cover the carpeted floor. Like tiny streaks of lightning they are strewn at all angles, discarded and left behind after a storm of feet carrying the latest fashions have passed through. Some of the pins have a swirly coloured ball on the end so they rest snugly in the mouth. But these lie contentedly side by side with their plainer counterparts and the children who cheekily lift the gilt letterbox over a hundred years ago are always treated to this shiny sight.

As a child, I was no different. In the tangle of my memories I looked through the letterbox on what had once been Madame Clapham's front door, staring down to the ocean of blue carpet with these slim silver pins bobbing haphazardly on the surface. It was intriguing and in my childish way, I wondered how painful it would be to try and walk across all those pins and why no-one had bothered to put them in a pin-cushion...

I liked her name, it was easy to pronounce and sounded like something out of a storybook. "Madame Clapham was a very important dressmaker from Hull," my Class 3 teacher announced. Clearly, her name was easy to remember as the name of Clapham spread throughout the East Riding and eventually the country amongst upper class fashionable ladies.

Madame Clapham was a distinguished, talented and famous dressmaker from Hull. She sold dresses to the rich, the royal family and even to women overseas whom she had never met. Her house and business address was number 1 Kingston Square, overlooking what is now the Hull New Theatre and previously the Assembly Rooms where even Charles Dickens had read aloud his work. It seems important to note that Hull was firmly on the map during the latter stages of the 19th century. The rapidly expanding fishing industry and booming business across the town meant that the ladies of Hull could aspire to look like the Parisian and London fashionistas of the time. It was Madame Clapham who would cater to their needs.

But how did this appeal to a seven year old in the mid 1980s? Well, we were taken to Kingston Square to "draw Madame Clapham's house as part of our Victorian Life topic" our teacher told us. Like many little girls, I had an innate ability to conjure up girl-ish fantasies and it did not take me long to imagine the stiff-backed, corseted, well-heeled Victorian women we had read about. I envisaged them entering into Madame Clapham's salon, to have the latest fashion of the day made for them, original stitch by original stitch in the sewing rooms on the first floor. It was November when we went and the wind would whirl around us, numbing my chubby little hand. I tried my hardest to capture a likeness of the grandiose house with my yellow and black school-issued Staedtler HB pencil with a shiny red tip.

With the last of autumn's red, brown and gold leaves blowing around our feet, I could picture Victorian women with fur-collared dresses, their hands placed in winter muffs, strutting up the steps to the front door. I spent an age trying to get this imposing black door right in my drawing; it was important to me because of what it led to. Like the nouveau-riche Victorian women gliding up the well-scrubbed steps, we all had one thing in common: we all wanted to see Madame Clapham's latest designs but had to cross this conspiratorial black portal first.

So, with a quick gasp of cold air and ensuring my duffel coat is presentable, let's delve into a seven year old girl's imagination and accompany one of these most respectable Victorian ladies into Madame Clapham's world-renowned salon and see these latest creations. Upon reaching the foot of the steps, I am swamped by petticoats and layers of satin. This is indeed a very "well-heeled lady indeed" I tell myself, repeating the words of my teacher. The lady does not notice the petite child peeking round as she knocks on the magnificent door which gleams in the late November sun. I am seemingly as invisible as the Emperor's New Clothes.

It is opened by an older lady who scrutinises the knocker before she clearly recognises the visitor and a smile breaks upon her face. However, even the young me can see that the smile does not reach her eyes. Yet this is not the eponymous Madame Clapham, it is merely a maid who will lead us through to the salon. How do I know? This woman's dress is formal but has none of the carefully cut lines or intricate needlework of a Madame Clapham design. We enter into the hallway and the pins are lazily scattered about but there are less of them than I witnessed through the letterbox and I resist an urge to bend down, pick one up and pop its colourful end into my mouth…

Listening carefully, I can hear the girls working upstairs but there is no conversation allowed. They respect this command and very little noise can be heard whatsoever…

Trotting through the blue carpeted hallway the more I learnt about Hull's famous dressmaker, the more things made sense to me. Born Emily MacVitie in Cheltenham in 1856 our young entrepreneur had begun her career by picking up pins from the workshop floor whilst completing her dressmaking apprenticeship in Scarborough at the then well-known Marshall and Snelgrove's department store. Although this must have been tedious work, the young Emily was not to be put off. An able worker who did not need to be told anything twice, Emily perfected her skill and knowledge of dressmaking. She knew how to match style with colour and emerged an utterly able and impressive seamstress. This self-belief clearly shone through and her husband, Haigh Clapham, who clearly believed in her too, used all their savings to buy No 1, Kingston Square in 1887. Madame Clapham was a tough, focused businesswoman who allowed pins to litter the entire stretch of her hallway which she could then pick up and use when necessary. They were sharp and so was she.

She placed an elaborate signboard above the door of Number 1, Kingston Square, announcing her presence to the women of Hull which was undoubtedly met by some scepticism in a town not readily associated with the height of fashion. However, the new Madame Clapham was not deterred. Surely some self-aggrandisement is necessary in order to find success in such a fickle field?

Self-exaggeration helped to ensure that over the next 4 years the premises of No 2 Kingston Square were also purchased to help accommodate the rapidly expanding business. By the start of World War 1, No 3 had also been added to the Clapham's property portfolio employing at its peak 150 people. The first three yellow brick houses of Kingston Square were now synonymous with glitz and glamour. During this time, Madame Clapham would visit nearby towns such as York and Harrogate meeting prospective clients whilst also making sure she travelled to Paris in order to keep up to date with the latest fashions. It seems incongruous, even today, that a woman based in Hull was having such an impact in such a notoriously prestigious and difficult to penetrate arena. Yet Madame Clapham's business acumen meant that she understood society; she knew what young women wanted, where they went and that what they wore linked directly to how they were perceived. Her dresses helped to ensure only a swan-like coming out for rich girlish patrons, there were to be no ugly ducklings in a Madame Clapham design...

My rich Victorian lady (with me following) is ushered into the front room to admire mannequins draped in silk, satin, lace and velvet as well as an actual model parading in and out to show us the latest designs. I sit cross-legged on the floor whilst Madame Clapham's client sits perched on the edge of an expensive upholstered sofa. We have been told in school that Madame Clapham only ever used the finest materials and accessories on her clothes so I am excited to see what is on offer today. White is still very popular (during the summertime especially) and fashion still catered primarily for the Lady who was sophisticated, from a respectable family and possessed a certain maturity. Glancing over to the lady I am accompanying, a wedding ring gleams on her finger and although 'young' by modern standards, she is clearly not a Victorian 'young' girl. Madame Clapham made sure that all her clients were looked after when they visited her salon and treated to the finest service that ladies of this calibre would expect. I wonder if it is time for afternoon tea...

Tea is served in the finest china whilst we wait. Little pastel-coloured cakes are neatly stacked on a tiered cake stand which my lady studiously ignores. She must know of the rumours that ladies in possession of a wide girth are apparently mocked by the sewing girls upstairs to the tune of 'Once round the waist, twice round Hyde Park!' (Markham, 118). Suddenly a model enters dressed in folds of silk with a heavily pleated skirt. This is what I have come to see! My Victorian lady's face glows with excitement. Then Madame Clapham enters and just like me, you are no doubt wondering what she looked like and how she dressed, no?

Her own sense of fashion seemed muted yet made a strong statement. It was reported she only ever wore black or navy and the very lining of her dresses was fragranced with lavender, leaving a lilac scented haze whenever she passed through a room. All her dresses had a train, rustling as she moved like the autumn leaves blowing about outside. She had an imposing physical presence with blonde hair and piercing blue eyes which no doubt added to her reputed icy persona. Madame Clapham had an eye for fashion because no detail, no matter how small, was ever over-looked and I can see that now: the eyes roving over the customer, no aspect left unchecked. Yet the glamorous high society visited No1 and 2 Kingston Square frequently, enjoying the expensive deep carpets and the well-matched curtains and sofas that exuded class and tasteful elegance. This helped to ensure that the name, address and designs of Madame Clapham were well sought-after.

The young Victoriana has an eye for the dress on the model and is told in no uncertain terms that measurements will be taken and to return in two weeks' time. Craning my little neck, I get a glimpse of the fitting room, adjacent to the sumptuous salon with floor to ceiling mirrors so no angle is left unseen. She is reminded to bring the accessories and jewellery she intends on wearing with this dress so that any further necessary adjustments can be made whilst bearing this in mind. I assume that this is how all dress-makers work yet it is to be another twenty five years before I am told to bring my accessories and jewellery to a dress fitting - perhaps the most important dress I will ever wear: my wedding dress. The dress in front of my little girl eyes to which so much scrutiny and care will be applied is probably just for a local ball...

Local balls were seen as a rite of passage by all of Hull's young stylish ladies and many a dress worn to such prestigious occasions was the creation of Madame Clapham. Existing in a time of 'coming out' seasons, hunt balls and glittering dinner parties, Emily Clapham was never short of work. One overjoyed seventeen year old spoke of how:

'Today I went with mamma to Hull for the day to get a coming out frock!! Oh joy, oh joy!! Girls brought in soft piles of silk and satin to exhibit to me. The satin frock has a very simple body draped with gold embroidery. It ought to be perfectly lovely we think.' (Markham, 117).

Such comments were indubitably common amongst Madame Clapham's youngest fans and this girl's fervour for the fashion is easy to hear. My Victorian lady is currently clapping her hands in an effusive manner as further examples of gentle alterations are made to the dress which is still being carefully modelled for her.

However, as my childish attention inevitably wanes, I see a copy of a magazine called *Hull Lady* sitting on a polished table top. There is a quote on the front from Madame Clapham explaining in typical, trademark confidence that 'To give you some idea as to the large connection I have... I may tell you I make dresses for most of the county and leading society ladies, also a great many for royalty, and I send dresses out to ladies living abroad whom I have never seen.' (Markham, 116). Her dresses were exclusive and always original. The quality was on a par with any large fashion house in London. And, to put it simply: her designs were beautiful. The year is clearly printed on the front of the magazine: 1901, around the time that Madame Clapham was at her zenith.

To celebrate reaching such dizzy fashion heights, by 1901 her clothes' labels and an alteration to the gilded sign above the door informed purchasers that she was The Court Dressmaker, designing dresses for the female royals and ladies-in-waiting.

Her most famous royal patron was Queen Maud of Norway who was the daughter of King Edward VII. Madame Clapham and her assistants were frequently called to London to dress the young Queen and the Hull dressmaker became a recognised face at Sandringham. She dressed countesses and viscounts but never forgot her Hull-based clientele, making the ladies of the city feel just as valued as the Queen of Norway herself. Indeed, one of her most influential Hull clients was a Muriel Wilson, the daughter of a shipping magnate in Hull, and her affiliation with Madame Clapham helped to secure business all over the East Riding and further afield. Today, if you are to pay a visit to Ferens Art Gallery there is a genuinely exquisite picture of the young Miss Wilson dressed lavishly in an original Madame Clapham dress made of silk ivory. Madame Clapham was an astute businesswoman, targeting influential local women and offering cheaper quotes than her London counterparts in order to win clients and dress-making deals. Watching her move around the room she reminds me of a matriarchal mother hen, pecking away at the fashionable desires of women.

Suddenly bored of the endless pinning and fitting that is going on before my eyes I turn my attention to what is happening upstairs in the sewing rooms. I stand up, move cautiously out of the rooms and scuttle upstairs like a little beetle in my navy blue duffel coat. Turning right at the top of the stairs I peer into one of the large workrooms. Girls are bent over their work, each one focused intently on what she is doing. Most are young, on a seven year contract which will then be reviewed with some kept on, some not. To work here gave a young seamstress in the city kudos amongst family and friends; she perhaps believed she was on her way to becoming somebody with the trips to dress royalty and the bourgeoisie and even if not, it would give her a story to tell. I remember being told that the girls who worked here normally came from quite well-off families as they would not get paid for the first year and had to be satisfied with their luck at being employed in such a famous emporium as enough compensation for going without twelve months' pay. Even to an untrained eye and my naive one, it is clear that there is a pecking order. The newer workers pick up pins from the floor and replenish pincushions (a task I fancy having a go at!), roll up swathes of material or make minor, basic alterations to dresses. The longer-serving girls work in 'teams' in specific workrooms, focusing on an exact item of clothing such as a skirt, corset, coat and sleeve or embroidery. Our teacher told us that apparently underage girls were hidden in cupboards when inspectors visited but everyone here is hard at work and I find it hard to believe that the rigid Madame Clapham would allow such a thing! The whole operation reminds me of a finely spun spider web, intricate pieces are being woven together as part of a larger design and it is all balanced gently, strung like invisible gossamer across several quiet rooms. I am awed by the silence and suddenly, the cold.

Yes, the cold. Upstairs is a world away from the luxury I have witnessed downstairs, there is no comfort from draughts here and in winter, freezing currents race up and down the long wooden tables placed in the centre of the workrooms. The floors possess no resemblance to their carpeted counterparts downstairs and are bare (apart from the omnipresent pins lying where they have fallen like wounded soldiers on a battlefield, having been beaten by others to hold in place a line on a new design). My shiny Clarks patent shoes stick a little to the newly scrubbed floor and as I rock backwards and forwards to offset the cold up here, I feel a sharp stabbing pain in my left thin rubber sole as a discarded pin pierces it.

Limping into the final workroom, I notice that there are hardly any machines being used although from my knowledge of Victorian life, impressive sewing machines were widely available at this time. However, Madame Clapham's apprenticeships sew nearly exclusively by hand, eschewing more modern dress-making tools except for flat irons which I remember our teacher telling us were known as 'gooses' because of the curve in the handle looking like a goose's neck. It made me chuckle but I can see why it had its name. Despite the austere surroundings, the girls are clearly enjoying their work; the opportunity to have access to such beautiful materials is not to be underestimated. Standing on my tiptoes and ignoring the flash of pain in my left foot, it is almost lunch-time - the only break these girls get - yet not one is checking the clock. We have missed our afternoon playtime to come here today but we did have the morning one at least. All sewers are engrossed in their work and are quick to jump to the aid of a fellow seamstress if she accidentally pricks her fingers and a spot of blood stains a potential royal garment! I glance down the stairs behind me but know there is little chance of Madame Clapham coming up: rarely did she interact with the young assistants she employed.

She was a tough and firm employer, the spider at the centre of the web. She was a straight-talker who did not waste words with her working girls. As we already know, all the Clapham workers had contracts that, if successfully kept on after an initial probationary year, were extended for a further six years meaning work was guaranteed for them. Many girls were 'let go' after the elapse of seven years in order to keep all the seamstresses focused and striving for the best in their work. Glancing around, this helps to explain the studious quiet and relentless conscientious attitude of the girls in the various workrooms. Even I daren't make a sound. I wonder who is coming to the end of their seven years and if the fine lines on certain faces are etched there through worry or sheer concentration...

Yet this is still 1901 and the Clapham entourage at its height. The girls work feverishly to produce stunning garments for the young and rich of Hull as well as the royalty of Europe. Gold is especially popular this season and flashes of brocade light up the dull sewing rooms casting thread-induced sunbeams across the clean floors and whitewashed walls.

However, it is a success that wanes over the coming years. Like an orchid that at first bursts with flowers, the petals of the business began to droop and wilt. Two World Wars saw a change in fashion, social freedom and the previous ability to obtain expensive fabrics. Made-to-measure designs were no longer *de rigeur* amongst the upper classes. The 1920s brought a vast change in fashion that even Hull's first couture dressmaker could not have foreseen. Many of the girls working upstairs, if lucky enough to be kept on after their seven year 'trial', would not be kept on after the war or were placed on part-time contracts. The demand for elaborate Victorian dresses was simply no longer there (although the older generation refused to move with the shortened-hem times and still placed traditional orders with Madame Clapham). It seems sad that the business had to contract but times were changing. Clients wanted clothes that were *prêt-a-porter*, they did not want to have to come in and have measurements taken anymore. Madame Clapham did sell some ready-to-wear clothing to London fashion houses but it was not enough to stop the decline. Like a delicate feather finally coming to rest on bare wooden floorboards, Hull's peacock of fashion had strut her last amidst the high-flying fashion flock.

It is time for me to leave, I have seen enough and thanks to my teacher, I know how this story ends. Hurrying down the stairs, ignoring my painful foot I look longingly into the front room once again. Stately clothes are still laid out and the smell of lavender becomes stronger as the great woman herself turns in my direction. She pauses, ice blue eyes fixed on mine. Freezing droplets sluice down my spine but she cannot really see me can she? My young Victorian is examining a sample of lace and Madame Clapham turns to give her a final nod of approval. The bill will be sent to the girl's father or husband; Madame Clapham is a real stickler for social conventions and would not dream of charging one of her female clients directly. Struggling with the heavy front door of No 1 Kingston Square, I slip through the gap and trip down the daunting stairs... never to re-enter Madame Clapham's domain again.

Despite the fashion empire of Kingston Square being rocked by social changes beyond anyone's control, the business managed to survive and Madame Clapham lived to be an austere, older woman, dying in her nineties in 1952 in her house in Kingston Square, leaving her niece to continue the business until it finally closed due to her death in 1967.

Sketching her house in pencil on a blustery November day, my immature hand was never quite able to recapture the grandeur and gorgeousness that house had once possessed. The large, high sash windows with their dividing pillars, the black balustrade and the neatly tiled roof were beyond my artistic grasp. I could not recreate Madame Clapham's establishment with any real sentiment. And it seems that neither could Hull City Council as it allowed her property to be bought in 1987 and made into The Kingston Theatre Hotel which is trading today; with only a restaurant inside aptly named The Clapham Restaurant paying tribute to the woman who brought couture to our town. The Hull Museum Service also owns some of Madame Clapham's original designs which can be seen in exhibitions from time to time. The grown up me has not visited the restaurant or been to a Madame Clapham exhibition. Something stops me. Perhaps it comes down to this: nothing will ever live up to the vivid, colourful memories of twenty-six years ago. The dresses shown in the exhibition will now be jaded, frayed and old-fashioned. In Kingston Square there will be no opulent fitting room, no sparse workrooms filled with activity, no materials on show in the front salon. And lastly, the harsh face of adulthood will reveal one final, horrid truth which I cannot bear to see. For I know, that ultimately, the hallway will now be free of the pins that had so glittered and gleamed, enticing a seven year old child over two decades ago.

Bibliography
Markham, Len. 2003. 'Dressmaker to the Queen', in Len Markham, ed. 2008. *Great Hull Stories*. Ayr: Fort Publishing Ltd, pp. 114-120.

'Hull Museums Collection Madame Clapham: Hull's Celebrated Dressmaker' http://www.hullcc.gov.uk/museumcollections/collections/storydetail.php?irn=405&master=454, [accessed 4/3/2012].

Humber Buildings

Mike Gower

We growl to a halt before the familiar vista of soot-blanketed walls, their powdered black contrasted with an occasional mildewed green. I grab the radio handset and thumb the speak button. "XT – Alpha-one-one in attendance – Humber Buildings - Madeley Street - Over."

Humber Buildings. Humber bleeding Buildings, society's discard bin. Believe me, Hull was enriched when the Hessle Road Flyover stomped every last trace into history back in the mid-eighties. If you had to attend a job there, you wanted a real fire, something hotter than hell. Hot enough to kill all the invisible things that treated you to days of constant itching you couldn't shower away.

Humber Buildings was the type of place that exists solely to remind the rest of us to count our blessings. In the early 1900s, it was a solution to the slum-housing problem. In the 1980s, it was just another part of the problem, one more cluttered group of semi-derelict maisonettes with enough inherent faults to have earned the architect a major design award.

And yet, there were those who called it home.

It's not unusual to be turned out to a chimney fire and arrive to find flames coming out of every window. Not this time, however. Before my boots touch the threadbare asphalt of the pavement, I'm already confident of that. I can see nothing worse than the odd spark sputtering in the smoke eructing from the chimney. More significant is that all I can smell is the sooty odour of smoking chimney. An experienced firefighter can smell a house fire two streets away. A good firefighter can tell you what's burning. I can smell soot, but with none of the acrid nuances of burning furniture or paintwork.

There's nobody around to greet us. I don't waste time looking around for whoever made the call. The locals can be quite shy in the presence of any sort of uniform, even one with yellow plastic leggings and rubber boots.

"Get your BA sets off, lads." They won't need them now, and there's no point in carrying fifty pounds of compressed air around on your back just for the hell of it.

This isn't my first time at Humber Buildings. I'm really, really not looking forward to going inside, so while I'm not exactly delaying, I am being very diligent about taking stock of the situation and noting all the necessary details. I pace out the asphalt desert around our target building. There are no flowers, no gardens. Landscaping around here follows the burnt-out car and disembowelled sofa tradition. The only indication of life is the chimney's smoky effluence. Scanning the building one last time, I put my notebook away and draw in a last deep breath of the crisp afternoon air.

It's time to go inside.

In the 1980s a good percentage of our domestic fires involved the sort of places where you wiped your feet as you left – and not always because of the fire damage. This was no coincidence. One of the many things the real poor can't afford is safety.

We were under no illusions; real people don't live in shop window displays. For the most part, we didn't discuss what we saw. We just did our job as best we could. Humber Buildings was different. It was in a league of its own. It was a prime example of 'don't care in the community'.

I leave the driver outside to monitor the radio, and to make sure that we still have wheels when we come back. The rest of us enter the building, laden down with equipment. Once past the concrete stairs leading to the upstairs dwelling, the narrowness of the passageway

True-life Tales from Sixteen Writers

forces us into single file, like emissaries bearing gifts to an ancient king. In the confined space I can't avoid brushing against the tiled wall. It leaves a greasy mark on my sleeve.

There's a pungent smell coming from somewhere. I'm not looking forward to meeting its maker.

Now we've reached our target maisonette. I don't need to worry about the front door being locked, not once I see the gaping hole where the lock should be. At my push the door grates open on strained hinges. I shout, "Hello, Fire Brigade," and step inside. Immediately the stench assaults me and it's so powerful that I can taste it. I feel an irrational need to hold my breath to stop the smell creeping into my stomach.

The hallway is elongated with nicotine-yellow walls, ceiling infested with black mould; even gloomier than the passage outside. Old instinct causes me to quickly scan for obstacles at foot level, in case we need to make a speedy exit later. I'm guessing from the few visible remnants of a pattern that there's lino down there somewhere, but I'm not enough of an archaeologist to want to find out. Either the occupant has a really big dog or that's human excrement all over the floor.

There is no response to my hail. I switch on my torch to identify the less noxious places to step. We press on towards the equally squalid living room. Once there I find that almost no natural light finds its way into the room through the slimy net curtains. Tearing them down wouldn't help much. I'm not convinced that the late afternoon light can fight its way through the mould and filth colonising the window.

It smells just as bad in here but by now I've breathed it in enough times that it doesn't dominate all of my senses. I'm reasonably sure that I can manage not to vomit.

I take a step forward and I'm looking down at a table, piled with soiled pots and festering food remnants. An enormous black cat, wedged into a space between a broken teapot and an encrusted dinner plate, is snoring away a bloated stomach. A smaller cat rummages through the shredded remains of a foil container.

I ease past the table. In the fireplace, the ruddy-orange light from a roaring fire imparts a cheery note, a deceit very much out of tune with the reality of the environment. Oddments of knotty wood, the kind that people scavenge from skips, are banked high in the grate, precariously high.

In a last-ditch battle against combustion, resin from the knots shoots a furious salvo of sparks into the smoke that's surging up the chimney. From time to time a knot bursts with enough ferocity to send smoke skulking back into the room, excreting a fine layer of soot over everything it meets.

Then I realise that the room is occupied. Next to the fire, close enough to become part of it, if any of the burning wood topples into the hearth, is an antiquated armchair, one step away from firewood. The occupant is equally antiquated - and if we don't do something about it, equally likely to feed the flames.

I have to look closely to make out the emaciated figure shrinking into the shadows. I step forward and he hunches even further back into the chair. I can see his head now, taut skin peppered with liver spots, clearly visible even through the grime. Shaking fingers brush self-consciously at the front of his tattered cardigan, gleaming with years of greasy food stains.

The old man's sunken, bloodshot eyes peer up at me. I step closer and the eyes wince shut, his face screwed up as if anticipating a blow. He tries to speak but it comes out as a wheezy indecipherable moan.

"Don't worry." I'm trying my best to speak without inhaling, "We're here to help."

He's somewhat, but not completely, reassured. With a noise like a creaking door, the old man pulls himself erect in his chair. The effort sends him into a fit of coughing. Gasping asthmatically, he fights to regain his breath. Mustering all the dignity he can, he makes one last request.

"You'll not make a mess, will you?"

If this story was fiction, it should end there on that line. After all, the place is long since gone. But when I look around me today, I can't help wondering whether what we buried beneath the flyover was the actual disease or merely a symptom.

Writing *Hull*

Barbarians In Rome

Nick Chapman

The number fifteen rolls by filled with eyes looking out into the middle distance, none of them quite appreciating what it is they pass.

To the right is a covered market of sorts, a dumpy looking building fronted by corrugated steel and graffiti. Inside are a number of modest businesses of varying types, from a Wicca crystal shop to a corner full of old LP's. It is not a thriving hub of commerce.

To the left is the staccato pulse of Newland Avenue; a bakers, a butchers and a bookies all crowded with Saturday shoppers, all too lost in their own personal concerns to take a minute and consider what is hung in their midst.

Nestled behind a screen of protective plastic, on a brick wall of little consequence, is a piece of history; an article that belongs more in a museum than it does in this cultural cul-de-sac. "For God, King and Country," the bold legend declares, "Sharp Street Roll of Honour."

Five portraits, faded with time, gaze off from the carved wooden frame with a noble bearing. Below the legend and within the fixed doors are over two hundred names elegantly gilt into the wood. I stop and see it for the first time. In three years of living in this city, in these streets, I'd never noticed this remnant of a bygone age.

There is no note nearby explaining this thing's arcane meaning, no helpful curator waiting to glide into place and reel off an expository spiel. Even the internet, that fantastic collective of knowledge, struggles to bring up any articles regarding the Sharp Street Roll. At best it reinforces my guess; that this is a list of local men who died in the First World War.

I'm not unfamiliar with war memorials, but why is one here? Why is it only a stone's throw from graffiti, steak and witchcraft?

Questions like this stay with me, fermenting as questions do, until I start asking them. Most who I ask are as surprised as me, had been as ignorant as me until now, had gone through life not knowing about the Sharp Street Roll. For some reason I feel this to be intrinsically wrong.

Then I tell my friend James and he only smiles.

"My dear boy," he brushes his moustache with the side of an index finger, "you need only to go into the town centre looking up, and you will be transported back in time."

"We have lost our way, you know." His look turns wistful. "We used to be great. Now we are as barbarians living in the ruins of Rome, calling ourselves Roman."

This is intriguing. It seems inconceivable that I could have lived in this city for three years and never looked up. Then again, it's also inconceivable that I should be ignorant of the Sharp Street Roll. So he takes me into town. And I look up.

And I see.

At eye level everything is new; new glass, new wood, new stone. The Paragon Interchange's regeneration seems to be complete, a transport hub for the twenty-first century. Buffeted along by a swelling tide of bodies I worry that renovators have replaced the irreplaceable.

Then my gaze travels up, and I'm transported back into Victoria's England.

The iconic glass and iron designs of the industrial revolution arc overhead in the roof of the train shed. Masonry, worn with time, threads down half a wall's length before being grafted into the new stone. A Frankensteinian union of past and future.

The tide of people goes out of the stations and splits into two streams, half flowing towards the great glass shopping centre to my left and the other towards the town proper. James moves towards the latter and I follow his lead.

Where my untrained eyes see only simple structures James can see the shimmer of time. Many buildings have the simple red-brick bearing of modern construction, no bells or whistles, but here and there are oddities which he highlights for me. The coltish awkwardness of sixties concrete, the errant slivers of wattle and daub public houses and a handful of elegant, pre-war constructions. Edwardian, he says, Victorian. Different sizes and colours of bricks tell him stories I cannot hear. Grand buildings with supporting pillars and embellished stone are usually owned by banks, he points out, as if to advertise their opulence.

On the right one building gives me pause. Mostly simple sandstone it is fronted by humble businesses. A cake shop, an army surplus and a travel agents; these are not today's movers and shakers. And yet, looking up, I see faces carved into the stone. No generic cherubs here, only faces of individuals, their names carved beneath. I recognise some of them and have to google the rest. Reynolds, Melsonier and Memling. Gainsbrough, Van Dyck and Titian. Lelasons, Lely and Rubens; painters all.

Why are these artistic giants carved into this building? I hurry forward, looking for the context, trying to understand why these simple shops share their frontage with artistic giants.

The great stone plinths and arches of the city hall tower proudly over the town centre, topped with a green copper dome. I don't even have to look up anymore. Across the way is the maritime museum, an example of equal age and prestige. A coffee shop works out of a building that still refers to itself as being the 'Yorkshire Penny Bank' and the shiny visage of Mr Punch grins down from his hotel. Victoria stands in the midst of them all, her marble gaze serious and scrutinizing of the mortals passing before her.

How could I have missed this? How could I have overlooked a square of buildings which have stood longer than living memory?

Realisation is slow, glacial in its momentum, but it comes. A stall is set up to the side, pledging to unlock mobile phones for reasonable rates. Charity buckets are raised hopefully in the direction of pedestrians who take a moment to tack their gazes to the horizon. A man with a fuzzy beard and a battered guitar strums an Oasis number off to the side. As a people we have claimed these buildings from our ancestors, adapted them to fit our needs, and lost something along the way.

Barbarians in Rome.

Tarmac gives way to rectangular cobblestones as Oldtown lives up to its name. Here a cathedral, its doors open to commune with its masses. There a 15th Century school, it's old, shifting bricks now a museum with an insight into Victorian life and ancient Egyptian death. And over there is the smallest window in England, its plaque valiantly drawing attention from the Land of Green Ginger.

I stumble on still looking up, wondering what else James could possibly have to show me. I'm about to suggest turning back when we arrive at our destination. A black wood front with gold embellishments and a hanging sign, at home outside any pub. It reads 'Hepworth Arcade' and claims to have been around since 1894. I'm intrigued; I didn't know they had slot machines back then.

Shiny tiled floors lead into glass fronted shops, each pane free of fingerprints and separated by marble pillars that travel up to an arching roof. It reminds me of the roof of the train station, but cleaner, not subjugated to decades of exhaust fumes. I can't recall ever seeing anything like it.

Again, I google. According to the internet Messrs. Mark and Spencer had one of their original penny bazaars in the arcade, before they got rich and moved down the road. Now it is almost exclusively independent businesses named after their founders, such as Dinsdale, Fanthorpe and Beasley.

In a corner I would have passed were it not for James is a curved glass wall that reads Hull Market Hall, 1904. This curved wall leads to a corridor full of named stores and stalls. Some sell t-shirts, others LP's. Some headstones, birthday cards, dogfood and drug paraphernalia. This corridor leads on to a massive hall filled with butchers, fishmongers and their like, all of them unknown to me until just now, trapped in a hidden sliver of time.

I wander around, gaping like a moon-eyed fool, until my phone shudders in receipt of an email, its contents relevant to what I could loosely dub as my mission in coming to town. I point James back towards the bus station and suggest we could stop by the Second World War monument on the way.

"Boer War," he is quick to correct, "or at least the statue is."

I feel shame creep up my neck and over my cheeks. Four years in the city and I've never once stopped to actually look at the memorial?

That changes today.

A grey feathered recon team stakes out the square. Their wings hunched up like shoulders, their bodies huddled against the cold, they look every bit like a browbeaten squadron hunkering down to escape the elements. They hop and scatter at our approach, flapping to circle overhead optimistically.

We start at the front, with the Boer statue James identified.

"Erected by public subscription…" I read the inscription aloud, trying to make sense of this alien concept.

"People used to have fundraisers," James waves at the impressive old stone, "fetes and the like, to pay for memorials such as this."

The unspoken accusation gleams in his eyes. The stone soldiers' features may become smoother, their rifles gather more rust with each passing rainstorm, but a hundred years on from their war theirs is the voice that speaks loudest. Theirs is the monument most memorable of the bunch.

When did dead soldiers stop warranting such remembrance?

We start a slow march around the memorial. The centre square is marked with marble plaques honouring the fallen from various units and conflicts. Eighth army, Royal Marines, Royal Navy, Arctic Convoy Veterans, those who were posthumously awarded the Victoria Cross and those who served in Burma and the Far East. All have the title of their war above a statement of respect and remembrance, all except the Korean War plaque of course. It speaks volumes for its reputation as 'the forgotten war' that its plaque is a slate of black marble with only the title of the war to show it happened at all.

The main memorial, a monolith of white stone, shows its age with its faded words remembering "The Great War and The World War." Poppies from Remembrance Day still litter the scene; wreaths of red from armed forces and their adjuncts line the back wall. Evidence, I suppose, that we have not slipped entirely into barbarism.

James rests his hand on the replica of a German advance milestone.

"From little towns in far off lands we came, to save our honour and a world aflame, and now by little towns in far off lands we sleep, so for what we fought is yours to keep."

I stare, astounded.

"Kipling," he sniffs and reluctantly removes his hand from the milestone. "Yours is the gift of words, is it not? You should write something about this."

A nod is the only answer I can give, and we continue back to the bus station.

The number one swings us back through town, back past the square where Victoria maintains her vigil, then away from town altogether. Past blocks of flats, under an overpass, we move closer to the corrugated warehouses of industry, on to Hessle Road.

The smell of fish and chips gets me as soon as I step off the bus, assaulting my senses. Hessle Road is worse than Sharp Street; a cultural backwater cut off from the life of the city through some unfortunate roll of chance. The mass of takeaways are only separated by the odd sex shop and hairdressers. In an unscheduled detour James and I explore a massive cash-and-carry selling pictures of Marilyn Monroe, teacups, soap and furniture. The escalators at the back of the shop whir to reluctant life as we approach, elevating us to a massive room filled with beds and tables and not one living soul.

Surreal doesn't cover it.

Back in the real world we finally manage to track down what I was sent here to find. James gives me a reproachful look as I guide him to Golden Town Chinese takeaway.

When I first started asking questions about the Sharp Street roll I'd asked my mother, who went away similarly stumped. With a more thorough search of the internet she'd managed to come up with better information, which she forwarded to me.

In the early years of the First World War an enthusiastic populace set up street shrines in remembrance of the local soldiers who died in the war. The death rate quickly outstripped the ability of local people to have the shrines updated, and after the Somme people stopped trying altogether. When the bombs of WW2 fell on Hull many of the shrines were lost; others were thrown away during the slum clearances of the 50s and the 60s. Allegedly there are five left in Hull. I can google locations for three of them and reasonably reach two of them.

The Hessle Street roll represents the last glimpse I can have into that bygone age, and I am somewhat underwhelmed.

Perched up high on the wall of a Chinese takeaway, written on simple stone, are thirteen names in three columns above a simple legend.

"Father in thy gracious keeping, leave us they servants sleeping," James muses on this.

A drunk staggers past loudly ranting at something only he can perceive and a man in the Chinese doorway notes that it must be noon.

James' request echoes in my ears as we catch the bus back into town, back to the safety of home where I'll have to put pen to paper.

I feel like Dilios ordered back to Sparta. How could I possibly do this justice? How can I put together the words that express the loss of life and the lost way of a people?

I'm paralyzed by the enormity of this quest. I stare at a screen for hours before the truth of the matter quietly makes itself known to me. I could never broach this subject in such a way as to make a difference. I could never write a piece that would have buildings revert to grander purposes, a piece that would transform a soldier's sacrifice from a half-forgotten waste to a nationally honoured celebration. All I can do is relate my short journey between two street shrines, and how my eyes were opened to the things hidden in plain sight.

Maybe that's enough.

Suicides and the Humber Bridge

Sarah Woods

With many thanks to the volunteers from Humber Rescue in appreciation of the work they do.

New Year's Eve 2004 Sherrie Smith was at a friend's party. Her fiancé, Lee Morgan, had come with her but decided to leave the party early. He had, as she later told the inquest, been in a "strange mood" and "looking for an argument over the silliest things". They had become engaged only a week earlier on Christmas Day and Lee had also recently been taken on as a full time employee at the bathroom company where he had been working as a casual. There is no suggestion he was drunk. Having told him to phone her in the morning, "when he had calmed down," Sherrie stayed at the party. She was looking forward to celebrating the New Year when her mobile rang. It was Lee. He said he was at the Humber Bridge and he was going to jump. Sherrie watched in disbelief as the video message played in her hands. The red warning lights of the Humber Bridge towers appeared on the screen bright against the black night sky. The lights came into view then disappeared, as the camera showed a rushing blackness. Then, the phone cut out.

    At twenty years of age Lee became one of more than two hundred people who have jumped, or fallen, to their deaths since the Humber Bridge opened in 1981. Built to link the two banks of the Humber, joining the socially and economically isolated communities of Hull and North Lincolnshire, the intention was to improve trade. A significant local tourist attraction the Humber Bridge was for sixteen years the longest single span suspension bridge in the world. It now appears to have received fame, or rather notoriety, as a suicide hotspot.

There is an international phenomenon of suicides occurring at public landmarks. San Francisco's Golden Gate Bridge is perhaps the most well known, with more than 1,200 people having jumped to their deaths since its opening in 1937. Of the two hundred people known to have fallen from the Humber Bridge only five have survived. Countless others have attempted to jump and either been talked down, or decided not to go ahead. But, what is it about the Humber Bridge that makes it such a popular place for suicides?

On a cold autumn morning I strode to the middle of the Humber Bridge to see what it was like for myself. Wind whipped at my hair and, the further I moved from the North bank the colder it felt. The main span of the Bridge is 1,410 metres and I positioned myself at the lowest dip of the wires halfway between the two towers. Traffic rumbled along the road behind me. Raised above the pathway cars and lorries travel at head height giving pedestrians an odd sense of disassociation and isolation. There wasn't another soul walking or cycling across the bridge on that autumn day. I turned to look down at the water. The cold metal fence pressed against my chest and I had to crane my neck. Anyone wanting to jump from the bridge would have to climb over this railing. The muddy water of the Humber slowly pulled and tugged more than 30 metres beneath me. It was mesmerising. Breathe, come on, and breathe, I told myself. I gripped tightly to the rail and snapped my head back. Vertigo, the sensation of falling, was both terrifying and yet compelling.

Living in the Hull, North Lincolnshire and East Yorkshire area it is impossible not to know, or know of, someone who has jumped from the Bridge. We may have no personal relationship with the people directly involved, but the local grapevine carries tragic tales. Beyond the suicides of people for whom the Bridge is a local landmark there is the question of suicide tourism. Two cases in particular were picked up by the media and publicised nationally. They illustrate this phenomenon and due to their shocking nature, as both involved a mother and child, are widely known.

On 10th June 2005 at approximately 9:30 the operators who man the Bridge's security cameras noticed something suspicious. They zoomed in. There, on the pedestrian pathway on the west side of the bridge, was an empty buggy and a child's shoe. Angela Schumann, 28, had wrapped herself around her daughter Lorraine, who was three days shy of her third birthday, and jumped from the bridge. Angela was in a state of despair following the breakdown of her marriage to Mexican born Julio Tumalan, whom she had met when seven months pregnant. There had been a long drawn out custody battle in which Angela had lost the day to day 'care and control' of her daughter Lorraine. Psychiatric reports produced at her trial stated that she was suffering, a 'depressive disorder' as a result of her lack of contact with her child.

The emergency call was made and the Humber Rescue boat was launched. Less than 44 minutes later mother and daughter had been found. They were pulled from the water, alive. Although only five people are known to have survived the fall from the Bridge the Humber Rescue incident report is typically understated about the matter. In the Incidents Report Log for June 2005 the entry for Incident 37 reads; "10.06.05 Humber Bridge jumper, mother and baby. Rescued and transferred by Heli to HRI."

Lorraine, protected by her mother's body, suffered only hypothermia and quickly recovered. Angela was seriously injured and remained in hospital for two months recovering from lower body fractures. On examination she was found to have scrawled on her stomach, "Cause of death, Julio."

The second incident which received widespread publicity and also involved a mother and child, took place on the 12th April 2006. Alison Davies travelled by train, from her home in Romiley near Stockport to Hull. She was accompanied by her twelve year old disabled son Ryan. It is known she took a taxi to the Humber Bridge. In an attempt to prevent 'suicide tourism', as early as 2001, Humberside

Police had written to cab drivers in the East Riding of Yorkshire asking them not to take 'distressed-looking passengers' to the Humber Bridge because of the high number of suicides that occur there.

The coroner's report shows Alison, aged forty-one, suffered from depression, a condition that had worsened since the break-up of her marriage. She had made three previous attempts on her own life. This single mother looked after her son Ryan, who suffered from Fragile X, a genetic condition, symptoms of which include behavioural and emotional problems with autistic-like features. Paediatrician, Peter Berchtold, speaking at the Coroner's inquest said, "It made him [Ryan] boisterous and demanding, and at the same time vulnerable and trusting. Ryan was completely oblivious to Alison's distress."

HGV driver, David Wilson, who was travelling from the south side of the river, witnessed Ms Davies holding her son over the barrier, as he drove past. This is how he described the incident. "He put his right arm over the barrier and then his leg and the other person was trying to lift him. As I got alongside, the child looked straight at me. We had eye contact and there was no distress, no fear on his face at all."

Dr Andrew Johnson, the family's GP, also speaking at the inquest, said Ryan had, "no sense of danger." And the Paediatrician, Peter Berchtold added, "it's possible he [Ryan] would not have thought past the adventure of flying." The coroner's verdict was that both had died by drowning, that Ryan had been unlawfully killed and his mother, Alison, had committed suicide.

Concerned by the rising number of suicides from the Humber Bridge a Scrutiny Report was undertaken in 2006. The combined forces of Hull Health and East Riding NHS looked into the matter. They found that nationally some 5,000 people take their own lives each year. Looking more closely at the figures they found that suicide is the leading cause of death in males aged 15-24 (a category that would include Lee Morgan) and that suicide is the principal cause of death amongst pregnant women. In conclusion, the Scrutiny Report recommended in December of 2009, that suicide 'hotlines' should be installed on the Bridge and the existing pedestrian barrier should be replaced by a much higher parapet.

Dr Richard Seiden of the University of California Berkley published, in 1978, a follow-up study looking at those prevented from committing suicide from the Golden Gate Bridge. He found that of 515 people stopped from jumping only 6% went on to commit suicide. Thus nullifying "[T]he major hypothesis under test, that Golden Gate Bridge attempters will surely and inexorably 'just go someplace else.'

The scheme, to raise the parapet, was costed at not more than £4.5 million. Peter Hill, Humber Bridge Master, speaking to *This is Hull and East Riding*, said, "10 years ago we couldn't have attempted a safety project of this type without compromising the structural integrity of the bridge. Through modern advances in modelling, manufacturing and wind tunnel testing we have now found a solution that will make the bridge safer for everyone." A trial section of 100m, still in place on the north side of the Bridge, has proved successful. It was hoped to see the erection of 6km of 2.3m high, inward slanting, hollow, aluminium poles. To date neither the raised barriers have been constructed nor emergency telephones installed.

Marcus, Outreach Director for Hull Samaritans speaking at the time of the report said, "We welcome the discussion around suicide and the Humber Bridge as the effects on the Bridge staff, as well as the families of suicide victims must be taken into account."

Indeed the effect of suicide is even more far reaching than he suggests. HGV driver David Wilson's moving eye witness account, given at the Davies' inquest, illustrates this point. And, apart from eye witnesses, there are those who work on the Bridge and those in the emergency services who attend these incidents. This includes a dedicated group of volunteers from the Humber Rescue. They are involved in initial call outs and the search and rescue mission that follows. It must be remembered that very few who jump from the bridge survive. Humber Rescue team members have the unenviable task of recovering the bodies. And, in many cases, the bodies are not located until sometime later.

Lee Morgan's body was not recovered from the river until the 9th February. He jumped to his death on the 31st December over a month earlier. It is known from witness reports that Alison Davies took her own life, and that of her son, on Wednesday 12th April 2006. Four days later, according to the Humber Rescue Incidents report, Ryan's body was found in the river at Swinefleet. He was discovered by a passer-by and eventually recovered some twenty miles upstream from the Bridge. The Humber Rescue team took his body to Blacktoft Jetty where they awaited the police and Undertakers. His mother's body was not recovered until 29th April when it was reported by a member of the public on the North Bank, again upstream, in the location of buoy number 33.

In addition to their role in retrieving the bodies of known jumpers, Humber Rescue teams also attend and record incidents where people are threatening to jump. In February 2006, the month Lee's body was recovered, the Humber Rescue boat was called to four other potential incidents. Fortunately, the would-be jumpers were successfully talked down from the Humber Bridge. It is difficult to find exact statistical information on potential suicides and these incident reports provide useful public information. Reporting is kept to a minimum to prevent 'copycat' suicides. The phenomenon, where someone seeks to emulate another's suicide, has become known as the Werther effect. This title comes from the novel by Johann Wolfgang von Goethe, *The Sorrows of Young Werther*, in which the hero takes his own life. The psychological effects of suicide are clearly far reaching but, I wondered, what is the effect on those directly involved? On a cold winter's evening I went to interview the volunteers of Humber Rescue.

"It's not something you get used to it's something you can either deal with or not," said Alan Stewart who has been with the crew since 2008. Dark haired and intense Alan, like the other members of the crew, works locally. His 'day job' is as a project manager. Sitting upstairs in the purpose built boat house, which resembles an oversized double garage, the volunteers chatted over mugs of tea. Every Monday night and Sunday morning the twenty volunteers who man (and in two cases 'woman') the fast-response rescue boat get together. They discuss their plans and practise their retrieval techniques using weighted dummies. Though, as Ian Bennett, Senior Crewman, Coxswain, Secretary and Manufacturing Technician pointed out, no-one was too keen on cold nights, such as this one.

"We've had highly trained people come and when they're faced with their first body well they're just out of here," said Dave Roberts the genial Chairman, Trustee and Coxswain. With a Father Christmas beard and twinkly blue eyes he quietly takes charge. He reminds everyone of the incident with Lee Morgan on New Year's Eve. "Everyone thought he'd just thrown his phone over. The whole family turned up, straight from parties, all in their cars. The police officer just took their keys off them and told them to go home."

It was a surprise for me to learn that they had anything to do with the victim's family. So I asked, what did the relatives want? "They come down and thank us, saying, we know you launched quickly but there was nothing you could do, but thank you," said Alan. "They're looking for answers trying to understand why their loved one jumped."

Everyone nodded their agreement.

"There was that recent one when his mother came and was asking, do you think he survived?" Ian raised his eyes to the heavens.

"Yes someone had told her he was seen swimming away," tutted Dave. "It's a 130 ft drop, they don't look pretty when they land. Some of them go straight down, get stuck in the sand banks and bob up weeks later." Ian and Simeon Hamilton, fellow Coxswain and instructor, pretended to hold their breath and made swimming motions with their arms.

"And we get our regulars too, come down to apologise for the trouble they've caused, or they can just be really distressed and that's when this comes in handy." Simeon waved his mug towards the small kitchen area in the purpose built Boat House. "We can offer tea and sympathy until the ambulance turns up."

Although there was an obvious good natured camaraderie it seemed likely that, at times, the work must prove distressing. Dave stared into his mug of tea for a moment before speaking. "Beverley was seven months pregnant when she jumped. She was in such a bad way when we pulled her out of the water. The first thing they did, when they got her to hospital, was a termination." Dave shook his head. "Well they patched her up and she just went again. Killed herself the second time."

This sad story, which was not reported in the press, is a salutary reminder to me. The shocking statistic of the 2006 Scrutiny Report that the most common cause of death amongst pregnant women is suicide.

"There was that lady that jumped, with her daughter!" Ian spoke up reminding us all of Angela Schumann and her two year old daughter Lorraine. "The little girl was about the same age as my daughter at the time." Ian shook his head. "I pulled them out of the water, but the mother was very bad, broken pelvis …it was very sad." There is an obvious sympathy from the volunteers which was not echoed by the authorities at the time.

In November 2006 Angela Schumann was prosecuted by the CPS and pleaded guilty to the attempted murder of her child. She was convicted and sentenced to 18 months. Nigel Cowgill, Humberside Chief Crown Prosecutor, said it had been in the public interest to prosecute. "[W]e made the decision to prosecute, because we felt it was important to fully record the actions of the defendant, which were calculated to take the life of a young child."

In response Prison Reform Trust Director, Juliet Lyon, said, "It is difficult to see what locking up this depressed, distressed mother will do to cut crime, respond to mental health needs or deter others from acting in desperation. Surely there is something better we can do to keep children safe and comfort tormented parents when relationships fall apart?" Angela's conviction was overturned on appeal.

I had noticed that the Humber rescue log shows the volunteers are called out to attend a lot of incidents on the Humber Bridge. I asked what this meant. Ian leant back in his chair his round face broke into a mischievous grin. "Oh yes, we're called out to a lot of incidents." This euphemism is used presumably to avoid the Werther effect. Fortunately, it would appear a lot of these incidents do not result in tragedy. I was interested to learn what role the volunteers played in these situations.

"Well we just sit in the boat and wait!" said Dave.

"Do you remember that time you waited 18 hours?" said Alan, and Dave nodded smiling. "That was back in the day. The police were bringing him pints of beer and everything just trying to talk him down. They've got wise to that now. If they're going to jump they jump straight away no messing."

"Yes," said Ian, "mostly the police get them if they're still on the bridge."

In the light of Alan's view, that those who intend to jump will do so, I wondered if they thought attending these incidents was a waste of their time.

"No. They're obviously not right or they wouldn't be doing it!" Alan answered immediately to vigorous nods of agreement from the crew. As Edwin Schneidman, co-founder of the American Association of Suicidology explains in his book, *The Suicidal Mind*, the cognitive state of suicide is ambivalence. That is, suicidal people "wish to die and they simultaneously wish to be rescued."

"We are on standby because if they jump they're whisked away. The river runs at 5mph," said Dave putting it into layman's terms for my benefit. "They can be carried up river or out to sea and never be found."

"Do you remember that Asian girl, we found her snagged on a buoy!" said Marcus, former RAF radio operator and police officer who has been with the Humber Rescue since 2003.

"Yes, she just walked into the river; you could see her foot prints where she was washed away," Dave nodded. "Even now, and it must be ten years, her mother can't touch anything in the house to do with her."

I wondered at what point in the call-out the volunteers would know if they are attending a rescue, a search, or an incident?

"Well, when a 999 call is made, it goes through to the Coastguard at Bridlington and then they page us. It's just a bleeper, with no information as to what the call-out is. As soon as you get the call you drop everything and get here as fast as you can. The first person to arrive checks in with the coastguard and he gives them the details. When the others arrive, two open the doors whilst two are getting their gear on. One person attaches the boat to the tractor and we're ready to launch."

The Boat House is conveniently situated, huddled under the Humber Bridge, set back from the foreshore on the North Bank of the river.

"If someone has already jumped the chopper will search in one area and we'll be directed to search in another. It all depends on the tides," said Alan.

I wondered if it was ever a hoax call.

"Oh it's very rarely a hoax," chided Ian. "We do get people who call us out like, do you remember that incident when the chap was peeing off the Bridge and someone thought he was a jumper?" There are chuckles of recognition all round. "Yes we call that a 'false alarm with good intent.'"

"A lot of them don't land in the water," mused Dave. "I was coming in one morning [bearing in mind the Boat House is beneath the bridge] and I could hear one crashing through the trees. I went out and there was a jacket caught on the railings, it had an arm in it. A dog walker found the rest of the body. There's still a bit of the jacket left on the railing I could show you if it wasn't so dark." He winked at me.

"And there was that woman that landed right underneath the upright," said Ian warming to the subject.

"And the parachutist who landed on the A63," said Simeon.

There were clearly many more tales to be told, but as everyone drained their mugs of tea I could see it was time to leave.

"Is that enough for you?" asked Dave. They had generously given up a lot of their time and I thanked them. Dave kindly showed me to my car.

We stepped out into the darkness on that cold December night. "You want to be careful. There are a lot of funny people about down here," he said pulling his cap firmly on his head.

There will always be those left behind who will wonder why and what they could have done to prevent a suicide. I thanked Dave, again, for taking the time to speak to me and he said, "Drop in whenever you like, we're here Monday nights and Sundays for training." Indeed they are on call 24 hours a day, 365 days a year, doing what they can when someone decides to commit suicide from the Humber Bridge.

As he walked back toward the warm glow of the Boat House I listened to the rustling of the trees' leaves and looked up. The red warning lights of the Bridge glowed brightly against the black sky and traffic rumbled along the road "from nowhere to nowhere". I hoped that no one was up there, on that windy path, contemplating a leap to oblivion.

Writing *Hull*

A View of East Yorkshire

Abby Harrison

"It's too flat," a man in a pub declared on hearing I was from East Yorkshire.

"But there's more sky," I replied.

Sky takes on a greater importance in East Yorkshire rather than just holding the weather as elsewhere. In East Yorkshire the clouds can be tracked, birds dance and the blue or greyness takes on gradients of hue that hills hide. The sun's blush or burn takes on the drama of a dawn or sunset in the desert. With a clear horizon each tree is already framed waiting for the wayward painter who has strayed too far from elsewhere to capture its shape. For there's a beauty in the flatness, like God had taken a roller to it. As a child I felt I could see forever, the world as limitless as the sky. You can see the Earth gently turn here. Elsewhere you have to don heavy boots, wear some ugly waterproof coat made socially acceptable by its label and climb a bloody big mountain to get that view. The only drawback is sledging, trying to find that perfect snow-covered hill could involve an excitement-draining car journey only to trundle down a gentle slope after a hefty shove. I didn't experience real sledging until I lived in Lancashire – there it was an extreme sport with an ambulance waiting ready at the bottom.

East Yorkshire isn't Humberside. Humberside ceased to exist in 1996, a twenty-two year label that still lingers in the national imagination and in the name of the local Police. It was even dismissed in Parliament as the Beverley MP James Cran said "almost the day after the decision was announced, a campaign began to have Humberside abolished." For across the river is different, a nearness not recognised by them or us.

The river is a mood repressor. When still, like a great brown mirror, it becalms, when rough, flecked with saliva, rabid, it's always angrier than you: valium for the teenager. You are insignificant, its mauling flow stronger than you. The suicide bridge a way out but not an attractive one – what if you survived? A mouth filled with mud.

You can go anywhere from here. Like when stood in front of the railway platform board in Milan the world is at your feet – you just need to make a decision. Travelling west, the hills don't tell you you've left, it's the chimneys of the huge chemical works. You've entered a little lip of North Yorkshire, like a referee standing between two boxers; East and West are held apart. And yet the land remains stretched out until it enters West Yorkshire when the first hills seem like unnatural sleeping giants, as they are – hints at the once strong but not forgotten industry underground.

It's agrarian land, the sheep would be suicidal on their bowling green fields if let loose. Small animals cower for it's a bird of prey's heaven. Dykes hidden by reeds form the only break, waiting for the drunken camper to visit for a nightmare night-time wee. Filled with water no one wants, like the dregs of saliva left at the bottom of a can. The land is fertile, sheep not needed to grow a profit, the land long ago drained. Clay lies underground, a fact I learnt at five when enquiring why Hull didn't have an underground system like London. And there's chalk; one of my father's favourite stories was playing at the chalk cliffs in Hessle with his brother and cousins and coming home with no backside to his pants from sliding down the slopes. Chalk quarrying was once a major industry with whiting taken across the world by boat.

To leave seemed necessary at eighteen. The sky was mocking, the horizon a gaping mouth. I was spat back a couple of times – failure in the outside world, only to venture again into the void. Hull has always been a place to leave and then return. For the fishermen, like my Grandfather who was met by the family on his return lest he spend all his wages at once, sailing the north around Greenland and

Iceland for fish or whales, returning was an event they all wished for.

Now I have come back voluntarily. My defence of the place working its magic on my own thoughts. My sister has travelled the world and lived in some of the most beautiful places on earth – the Lake District and New Zealand – and even she chose to return.

On mornings, arising in darkness the orange sky guides me to work. At night the pastel pink blush on powder blue silhouettes the houses. Everyone hurries by looking down, like New Yorkers oblivious to their manmade sky attractions which only tourists stand and stare at. My eyes are drawn to the sky, but not now as a promise of elsewhere as they're not there elsewhere!

Even Hockney's noticed, labelled our greatest living artist, he has returned from the light of California to the light of East Yorkshire, perhaps others will too. Seeing his paintings in London, some former residents commented they "make you want to go home." It's the "big skies" that have drawn him from the eternal sunshine, as well as the open spaces free from people.

Hockney is right, there is an emptiness about East Yorkshire. Villages are often sparsely spread, each keen to ignore their closeness to the metropolis of Hull. Even in the city's outskirts people are not inclined to describe their address as Hull, but the area name. Villages are described as "near Beverley", "on the way to York" or "near the coast". This is perhaps because the disparity between rich and poor is so pronounced. In Beverley an ASBO was placed on a young man who was told by the Police "Beverley is a place where posh people shop" who don't want to see congregating youths.

Yet even amongst the well-to-do the dialect is audible. In East Yorkshire language is free. Hullitos speak as if new to the language, as one lady said in a coffee shop when asked where the toilets were: "Upstairs. But don't use the front stairs – they are awfully steep. Use the ones at the back. The front stairs are suicidal." In their quiet way they are masters of understatement: "I don't particularly like the bloke, I mean I haven't spoken to him for twenty years." Perhaps Shakespeare visited. It must be the mix of cultures from the different nationalities arriving through the port over the years; people were always learning the language.

Journeys are a vital in East Yorkshire, yet all of the means of transport are flawed. Returning to Hull by road and the motorway becomes an 'A' road and the bridge only goes to Lincolnshire (not much there). To travel by ferry offers only grey seas, lorry drivers and generally grey skies at the other end. Even the railway line ends in Hull, as I was once told by a ticket collector, "If you don't get off in Hull you'll fall into the sea." I've always wondered whether the Bronze Age boats found at Ferriby were leaving or just arriving, drawn by the unknown.

Perhaps I won't stay. It seems churlish not to sample other skies. I hear Pakistan has a different moon.

When Adam met Fat Billy

Mike Gower

The story of Hull surely begins with Adam. No, not that Adam. Our Adam comes later, a mere thousand years ago by our calendar. As for Eve or serpents… well, this Adam has different passions.

Imagine a hill. Picture it in your mind as a real hill, not some feeble bump. This is a verdant breast of a hill, whose gentle inclinations nurture acres of pasture, stream, and woodland. This hill is where it all began for both Hull and a major part of East Yorkshire as we know it now. In a sense, it's also where a major part of our local history ends.

For the Adam of our imagination, it's beginning right now, in 1150 AD. Right here and now as the gentle breeze on the hill's crest tugs at his hair and stirs the folds in the plain wool of his robe.

I have to ask myself, as his gaze follows the movements of young deer playing chase the leader around the edge of the forest, "What does he know?" Again, as he studies the distant wisps seeping from the smokehouse of a tenant smallholder, "What can he know?" As he squints to take in the sodden fields lying close to the Humber, far beyond the southern base of our hill, I realise that the seed that is Adam can possess neither awareness nor understanding of the tree he is bringing into existence.

Beginnings are important. We need to go and find Adam on his hill, to see for ourselves. This is not an easy journey, a struggle for twentieth-century legs, an ordeal for twenty-first century imaginations. A car can ease the ease the strain on the leg muscles. As for the rest… we'll see.

We're heading through the north end of the city, risking our vehicle's suspension on the procession of sleeping policemen delegated to guard a ruler-straight road. The road bisects the eastern perimeter of what used to be the largest public housing estate in Europe, a town within a city by the name of Bransholme.

For the most part the buildings lining our route have accumulated less than fifty years of existence, no more than a mayfly's day in the sun compared to the grand scheme of things. Fleeting enough that our true vision, that of the imagination, can pierce their illusion of permanence, can see through to the generations of rich meadow feeding into generations of woollen wealth. With more effort we can see further back, to Adam's time, to the land's previous incarnation as soggy bottomland, as yet undrained. Rich in minerals. Richer in the lives of unwary travellers.

Our focus lost, we snap back to the present, passing a few larger houses holding themselves primly away from the roadside. These are slightly older buildings still grieving for the lost fields and meadows of their pre-war youth. They look lost, out of place, befuddled by their latest reincarnation as storage units for the elderly.

A standard issue school cowers, mute and expressionless, behind the chain link perimeter of its enclosure. It cringes away from the mayfly buzz of pebble-dashed people-hutches bunched around it, their scarred paintwork faded to the colour of old tattoos.

This land, rich land that for most of a millennium nourished the bellies and purses of a nation, has harvested only people during the eye-blink we regard as the recent past.

We continue onwards and upwards, leaving behind the estate houses as we pass several of a more public kind occupying the fringes of what our mindsight tells us were ancient game forests, once restricted to knightly pursuits. In twenty-first century Bransholme, the hunt pursues a different type of quarry on a nightly basis.

Accelerating, we speed past another momentary blip on the map that the signpost tells us is yet another housing estate, imaginatively known as North Bransholme. The village of Wawne, or Waghen as it called itself in its youth slides past almost unnoticed as the road suddenly twists and turns on itself, morphing into one of those

Moebius-twisted labyrinths that leave you in no doubt that you are following an English country lane.

Towering hedges block our present-day sight on both sides of the road. In 1150 AD there were no hedges, but our very proximity to Adam allows the mundanity of the present day to intrude, obscuring our mindsight. Until, that is, we reach a gap in the hedge. Suddenly sunlight shafts down through the clouds, spotlighting the patchwork land that flows from our sight towards the Humber, allowing us to catch a glimpse of the view that has bespelled Adam. It's only a tiny glimpse, but just for that single moment we can share with him. As we share, the hedges fade from view. Donning the wellington boots of our imagination, we trudge back a thousand years or so to join Adam.

Here we are; it's 1150 AD and we're standing on a plateau atop an immense grassy mound that falls gradually away southwards towards the wetlands that comprise most of the region between here and the Humber.

Right now, in 1150, locals call this place St Mary's Hill. From our vantage point on the hill we can make out miles of woods, orchards and plenty of fresh water, all below us on the hill. The soil at our feet is rich and well nourished; an indication that the lush acres rising up to meet us will make excellent pasture.

The hilltop covers such a large area that we can't see the westward slope. If we could, we would know that someone has already made a start on drainage. Off to the west side of the wetlands at the foot of the hill, there is a raised bank of earth and a broad ditch. The man responsible for this work is standing just a few yards away from us. He has only just acquired the land, which he thinks will make an excellent hunting park. If his companion has any say in the matter - and he does - the land will be used for another purpose entirely.

Let me introduce them. The owner of the land, the elderly, richly-dressed barrel of a man is William le Gros, Count of Albermarle, Earl of York and Lord of Holderness. With such a god-given match of form and nomenclature, his nickname is inevitable.

It's also inevitable that no man will ever call him Fat Billy to his face. Not for so long as he's the owner of the armed retinue that's loitering over there by the horses.

Don't worry, the bodyguards won't bother us. They're just doing what retinues always do: standing around, picking noses, scratching armpits and generally enjoying the late summer warmth.

You might think that the man wearing the plain, greyish-white, hooded robe, standing beside William, has the weathered face and calloused hands of a labourer. You'd be right to do so. Finally, we meet Adam. By trade, he's a monk-mason from Fountains Abbey. Adam's passion is for the construction of monasteries. He has already been involved in the founding and building of a number of these, including Kirkstead, Woburn and Vaudey. Adam's here to help William out with a bit of a problem.

William has pledged to undertake a pilgrimage to Jerusalem, a risky undertaking so soon after the failure of the Second Crusade in 1149. He is no spring chicken and his waistline is now very much in keeping with his name. His chances of returning intact from this pilgrimage are not great, but reneging on his pledge could cause him serious problems with the church.

William is however a man of his times and he has had previous experience of fixing these sorts of problems. In the 12th Century the unique selling point of the Christian faith was the principle of repentance and penance. Repent of your sins, pay a suitable penance and your soul can be once again spotless. William has already endowed two monasteries, so when he met Adam, who was helping to build the second of these, at Vaudey, he must have realised that he had found a man who had the right contacts.

Adam is a member of the Cistercian Order and asked, in return, for what any good Cistercian monk-mason would ask – land on which to build yet another monastery.

Let's not intrude on their argument. William is starting to look a little heated while Adam displays the serene expression of a man who knows that it's only a matter of time before he gets his way. They're speaking Norman French, the lingua franca of their time.

The gist is that William has his heart set on the hunting park which he bought so recently that the deeds haven't even been transferred to him yet, while Adam is more or less repeating words to the effect that God wants his house on this hilltop, so that's where it's going to be built. Like any good Cistercian, Adam knows his land.

William eventually has to give in and Adam gets the land, an area about four miles in circumference.

And that is the end of the beginning. It seems to be a meeting of seemingly small consequence to anyone but the participants. Yet without that meeting, without Adam's insistence on siting the new monastery at that precise location, the city of Hull may never have existed, and the landscape of that part of East Yorkshire known as Holderness would be vastly different.

We'll wave them goodbye for now because we need to trek just a little further to 1160 AD. It's not that far but on the way I'm afraid we're going to talk about religion.

In 12th Century England Christianity was still, relatively speaking, the new, albeit very powerful, faith on the block. This was especially so in the North of England, where your recent ancestors might have known more about Odin than the Jewish carpenter's son.

Early Christianity in Britain was full of zeal, energy, and ambition; and it pulled in dozens of different directions at once. Although all of Christianity owed allegiance to the same Pope, the individual organisations competed against each other like siblings. And just like siblings they often became embroiled in bitter rivalry, especially when money was at stake.

People have many reasons for joining organisations, even today. Twelfth century England's feudal society forced most people to belong to something or to someone. Social mobility within established society was rare and the Church provided one means of escape from serfdom for intelligent or enterprising individuals. In addition, the pan-geographic spread of the monastic organisations provided one of the few ways in which trade could bypass the intervention of local feudal lords. Bearing all that in mind, let's take a look at the Cistercians.

The Cistercians were (and still are for that matter) an international order of monks, originally formed in France. They are committed to strict observance of the rules for monastic life laid down by St. Benedict - a former Roman citizen who dropped out of school and lived in a cave for three years before coming up with the aforesaid rules. They say that the road to Hell is paved with good intentions and the intentions of the Cistercians were originally the very best, a simple life of austerity and prayer.

Doubtless many of the monks in the order remained as devout as you would expect from people who spent their lives in hard labour, were allowed only plain clothing and forbidden to shave more than once a month. However, the higher an individual stands in any organisation, the more he must deal with the outside world and the worldlier he becomes.

Since the time of William the Conqueror, England had been moving progressively away from the barter economy of the Saxons. By the later years of the twelfth century, money and its acquisition were hot topics on everybody's lips, especially within the higher echelons of the various religious communities.

By the time Cistercian monks arrived in England in 1118 AD, the mission statement encompassed a life of austerity, prayer and the relentless pursuit of profits for the use of their Order. Mostly they achieved the latter through a series of unprincipled and aggressive land-grabbing techniques that would have shamed a Wild West cattle baron. One English Justice of the period said that he always exempted Cistercians when pledging his oath to do justice to all men, since, "It is absurd to do justice to those who are just to none."

It's only fair to say in defence of the Cistercians and their brother and sister orders that, at the time, they were the only providers of social welfare to the poor, sick and elderly of their communities. Far from receiving financial backing from the government, the monasteries provided financial backing to the government. Cistercian monasteries, for example, were required, as part of their charter, to provide 'a strong prison in which criminals, such as thieves, incendiaries, forgers and homicides should be locked up at the pleasure of the Abbot' (Thomas Burton, 1396). All of this obviously had to be paid for somehow.

In the 12th Century, the wool trade was of enormous financial significance to England. English wool was in huge demand in Europe and the country as a whole became extremely wealthy from the export of wool to the other European countries.

The traditional way for landowners to produce an income from their land was to divide it up into lots of parcels for letting to small farmers. These people in turn grew crops for market and to meet their own food needs in addition to raising sheep, cows and pigs.

When Cistercians first arrived in England they quickly realised that the supreme cash crop was sheep. The Cistercians developed a corporate policy of, whenever possible, removing small farmers from the land that they acquired in order to turn it over to pasture for their own flocks. The practice did not make them universally popular.

Nevertheless, the Cistercians soon became the biggest wool-producers in the whole of England. This fact was of great significance for the future of a piece of wasteland known as The Wyke of Myton.

Here we are, safely arrived in 1160 AD. The grey-robed man who greets us is not Adam but Gerard, one of the Cistercian brethren of Meaux Abbey. He tells us that William Le Gros is very happy that Adam did manage to obtain a dispensation from Pope Eugenius III, releasing William from his pilgrimage vow – so happy that Adam became the first Abbot of Meaux Abbey.

Looking around we can see that Adam and his selected monks have been hard at work. Much of the land that we saw in 1150 AD is now criss-crossed with drainage dykes and a large, two-storey wooden building has been erected; the lower floor used as a dormitory and the upper floor a chapel.

Gerard tells us that the wood used in the construction came from the remains of a wooden Saxon castle, given to Adam for that purpose, and that all the work has been carried out by the monks themselves. With our advantage of 21st Century hindsight we already know that this wooden monastery building will in later years, after a stone monastery has been completed, be set to an equally worthy purpose – the monastery's brewery.

Much energy has also been devoted to the Cistercians favourite pastime – acquiring more land, much more. Meaux Abbey now owns at least thirteen hundred acres.

Adam, however, is much better at founding institutions than running them. Despite all the land acquisitions, Meaux never seems to be able to match the revenue generated for the Cistercians by some of the other Yorkshire monasteries. Of course, it doesn't help that reprobates from Swanland are stealing Meaux' sheep; or that the Abbey has been involved in a number of acrimonious legal disputes over land rights, in particular with Roger of Bishopsbridge, the Archbishop of York.

By the time we arrive here in 1160 AD, Adam has resigned his position as Abbot and left to live in another monastery. The first act of Adam's successor is to buy yet more land.

The new Abbot, Philip, is a much more worldly man than Adam. He has a plan. If the Cistercians had their own port, not only would they avoid all the fees that they currently have to pay to the port of Hedon when exporting their wool, but they could make extra profits from other wool producers in the vicinity.

Philip isn't here at Meaux right now. He's visiting a lady by the name of Matilda Camin, daughter of Hugh Camin, in connection with some soggy wasteland alongside the mouth of the River Hull; an area known locally as the Wyke of Myton.

The monks of Meaux know that the key factors in any land deal are location, location and location. For what they have in mind, this land ticks all the boxes for a port of their own, one with even better access to the Humber and North Sea than nearby Hedon. They are going to create the port of Wyke upon Hull.

It's time to wave goodbye to Gerard and head back to the Twenty-first Century. We'll talk on the way. Philip and his monks, as you probably know, succeeded in creating a port on the River Hull. This started yet another feud with the Archbishop of York, who claimed that he had the sole right to charge fees and levy taxes for the use of the river. In 1293 this became immaterial when Edward I made the monks an offer they couldn't refuse; and the place that people had started to call Port of Hull became officially King's Town upon Hull and a major military arsenal.

Meaux Abbey and its monks survived until the dissolution under Henry VIII, in 1538. They built and rebuilt the Abbey more than once. Sometimes they struggled and often they didn't; mostly they continued to be at loggerheads with the Archbishop of York, regardless of who occupied that role; sometimes violently so.

Their land acquisitions ranged as far afield as Goxhill, on the south bank of the Humber, and made them owners of virtually the whole of Holderness. They carried out drainage work on every piece of land they acquired, perhaps less successfully in the case of Ravenser Odd; which vanished beneath the Humber in the 15th Century.

There are those who say that water isn't all that was drained from Holderness. It can't be denied that the monks came up with a number of money-making schemes, some sensible, some less so. One of these involved the carving of a huge naked crucifix, using a live model, after obtaining dispensation to display the crucifix to devout women. They claimed that entertaining the women cost them more than they actually made from the viewings. Perhaps they were too far ahead of their time. Or maybe fiddling expenses isn't just the prerogative of modern-day politicians.

We can still see the legacy of Meaux Abbey in the network of dykes and ditches spanning the whole of the Holderness plain. If the land had never been united under a single, hardworking owner, it's debatable whether a drainage project on this scale would have been undertaken. Without Meaux Abbey and its monks, Holderness, including the City of Hull, might still consist mainly of fenland. Some parts might not exist at all.

Well, here we are - back home in the 21st Century. We're still at the site of Meaux Abbey. Take a look around. For over five hundred years this was the home of the people who created Holderness as we know it today. Five hundred years! Look back five hundred years from today and you find yourself before the English Civil War, before the beginning of the modern political system, before the majority of what we regard as British history.

We're in a field of long grass, surrounded at the perimeter by low trees. Under our feet is a long, low mound, perhaps two or three feet higher than the surrounding terrain. At the far end of the mound, a solitary, immense oak tree spreads its branches to provide a fitting headstone for our lost Abbey.

That is all there is for us to see here; the legacy of five hundred years of service to the community, or service from the community, depending on your viewpoint.

The Abbey was the religious, economic, legal, and social heart of Holderness for half a millennium. The results of the monk's hard work are visible everywhere in Holderness, even today. Yet not a single stone of their home remains. The stonework of Meaux Abbey was taken away to build the military Citadel, for the protection of Kingston upon Hull. That citadel has itself now long since disappeared.

It's time for us to depart. This land is now private property, belonging to a local farm. For five hundred years Melsa Abbey was the most significant power in Holderness. Local farmers rented land from the monks, if they were lucky. Today the very site of Melsa's main buildings belongs to a local farmer.

As we leave, we can see nothing to indicate the significance of this place. No nameplate. No historic monument road sign. Nothing.

Nothing but a mound of earth and a tree for a headstone.

Writing *Hull*

Hull's Royal Station Hotel & The Parapsychologist

Darren Lee Dobson

'Scratch beneath the surface of any city and you will unearth tales of paranormal activity,' began Mike Smith, the co-founder of Ghost Chasers UK.

He was thirty-five. He wore a light blue suit and a white shirt and a pair of round-rimmed spectacles, which he took off from time to time, as if scrutinising the world around him. His hair was cut short and was brown, with a peppering of light grey.

When he spoke, he spoke slowly, composing each sentence with care and punctuating them a dry chortle. He rocked forward conspiratorially when pet topics and serious points merited emphasis, but looked visibly relaxed as he sat back in the cushioned chair and sipped his black coffee.

'As a parapsychologist,' he continued, 'I try to look for rational explanations for unusual phenomena. Sometimes it's not always possible, but I always try to find one first. That is to say,' a thoughtful look crossed his face, 'at Ghost Chasers we approach all our investigations with an open mind and with the view that all things are possible. Integrity, professionalism and the pursuit of verifiable evidence of the paranormal is our dictum,' he smiled.

It was early evening - late October. Sodium light filtered through the main portico window of Hull's Royal Station Hotel. Shadows formed and pooled around the bold arches and potted ferns on the far side of the lobby. Overhead, fifteen tubular lampshades shone down and reflected in a soft hue of burnished bronze. The atmosphere - normally relaxing and serene - seemed more melancholy, somewhat like a watery sun trying to break through a heavy dawn.

But I wasn't there for street theatrics. I wanted to know what

Mike Smith and his work as a parapsychologist was all about. For my part, I had to admit that my picture of ghosts and their surroundings was a traditional one: a grove of dark forbidden laurels crowding the door of some ancient pile, mist swirling around the battlements, and inside the ubiquitous figure of a grey lady or a hooded monk floating along the dusty corridors, before disappearing through a solid brick wall. Outdated images, perhaps? Acquired from books I had long since read. There was also this about ghosts: they are usually pale or translucent; you glance away for a moment and they are gone; they are camera shy and are nearly always seen wearing clothes.

Mike describes himself as a travel advisor and paranormal investigator. During the day he works at the booking office in Hull's Paragon Interchange, selling train tickets and dispensing travelling advice. At night... well, that was another matter.

'Growing up in the 80s was an exciting time for me,' he went on thoughtfully, recalling the time he became interested in the paranormal. 'The TV was full of supernatural programs like *Tales of the Unexpected*, Arthur C. Clark and my favourite,' the corners of his mouth flickering slightly, as if remembering a dark and guilty secret, '*Sapphire and Steel*, with David McCallum and Joanna Lumley. I don't suppose you remember?' he added expectantly.

I shook my head.

From the other side of the hotel's kitchen door there came the distinctive sound of moving cutlery and glasses being stacked together. The door suddenly swung open and out came Christine, the head waitress. Carrying a tray filled with recently cleaned glasses her face brightened into a slow smile as she turned and spotted Mike.

'Can I have a word?' she said, sidling over. Her tone was dry and chalky.

'Of course,' Mike smiled and, with a subtle nod of his head, indicated that she could talk freely in front of me.

'It's happened again,' she said, lowering her voice into a whisper.

'Only, this time -' she went on, carefully leaning closer. '- Barbara, the cleaner, felt something push her in the back.'

'On the third floor?' said Mike matter of factly.

Christine nodded. 'It's getting so bad no one wants to go up there.'

Mike took a notebook and pen from his pocket and wrote down the somewhat sketchy details. 'Don't worry,' he said, leaning forward slightly. 'I'll investigate the matter further and get back to you.'

'Well, must be getting on, then,' said Christine, quietly reassured. 'No one likes a slow waitress, eh?' Skilfully balancing the tray in the upturned palm of her right hand, she hurried across to the bar where a bearded man had been waiting patiently.

'That's the point I was making,' said Mike, lowering his voice until Christine was out of earshot. 'At least one in seven people in the UK have had some sort of paranormal experience. And this -' He waved the notebook in the air as if it were a piece of crucial evidence. '- is just one of many ghost stories from up and down the country.'

Mike seemed to exude an energetic - if not, impatient - eagerness to help others understand the true nature of the paranormal. An eagerness sharpened only by his formal training, as he went on to explain: 'To become a parapsychologist, I did a six-month course with the Open College. Much of the work was online, apart from a couple of residential workshops, that is. There were...' He crumpled up his face as if doing a complex calculation, 'two written exams, if I recall and...a practical, much like any other diploma, really,' he concluded, jutting out his chin with an air of pride.

The hotel's main door was pushed open, letting in a cold blast of air and the sounds of the early evening rush hour. For a brief moment there was a glimpse of the outside world. The clouds had broken and half a moon filled the car park with cold silver and black. A middle-aged man stepped in off the street. He stood for a moment - a grey suitcase resting patiently by his side like an obedient dog

- took out a crumpled piece of paper from his pocket, checked it... and checked it again, before making his way over to the main desk.

Designed by George Townsend Andrews in 1851 the Royal Hotel is one of Hull's most famous and historically significant Victorian structures. Over the years a number of well know people have passed through its grand lobby.

On the 13th October 1854, Queen Victoria (reign, 1837 – 1901) stayed at the hotel with the prince consort and five of the royal children. It was said that when she stepped onto the balcony, she was moved to tears at the sight of 10,552 school children, accompanied by 1,210 teachers, being marched into the yard in front of the hotel and positioned on a series of raised steps, forming a vast amphitheatre.

During her stay Queen Victoria wrote a letter to the King of the Belgians (not the King of Belgium, as commonly known), Leopold George Christian Frederick, in which she warmly mentions her visit to Hull:

We left yesterday morning, slept at Holyrood last night, and came here this evening; the good people of this large port, have since two years entreated us to come here. We shall reach Windsor tomorrow...

In honour of Queen Victoria's visit the hotel was later renamed the Royal Station Hotel.

Some thirty-six years later, on the 18th February 1890, Frederick Bailey Deeming (conman, serial killer and bigamist) stayed at the hotel with his new wife Helen Matheson, of Beverley.

Not long after their arrival it was said that Deeming disappeared, taking his new wife's expensive jewellery. He also swindled £150 out of Reynoldson's jewellers, on Whitefriargate, before leaving the city.

Deeming was later arrested at Montevideo, Uruguay and charged with 'obtaining goods by false pretences' for which he was extradited back to Hull (the first known case) and received a nine month prison sentence.

Upon his release from Hull Prison Deeming visited his first wife Marie (nee James), in Birkenhead, Liverpool. He told her of his plans to travel to South America and promised to send for her and his then four children. Whilst in Merseyside, he also began courting a third woman Emily Lydia Mather, the daughter of a widowed local shopkeeper, and bigamously married her on 22 September 1891. Deeming and Emily left the UK for Australia.

After the publicity surrounding the discovery of Emily's body in Windsor, Melbourne, in March 1892, police in Liverpool lifted the floorboards of his former house and found the bodies of his first wife (Marie) and their four children; all five throats had been slashed.

Remarkably during his trail Deeming claimed insanity, on the grounds that he received visitations of his dead mother's spirit, which urged him to kill. The experts were divided and when sentenced to hang, Deeming turned to the court and declared all those present to be 'the ugliest race of people I've ever seen.'

What you might find surprising is that there are some who still believe Deeming to have been Jack the Ripper and that, whilst Helen slept at the Royal Station Hotel, he stalked the darkened streets of Hull, looking for his next victim.

More recently, Hull poet Philip Larkin wrote 'Friday Night at the Royal Station Hotel'. The hotel was said to be one of his favourite haunts. On the 2nd December 2010, to commemorate the 25th anniversary of his death, Hull City Council unveiled a 'larger-than-life', seven feet tall, dark green, bronze statue of the poet positioned near the hotel's station entrance. With a manuscript tucked under one arm and clutching a trilby in the other, his coat-tails flying behind him, it portrays an active face of a man more often pictured in repose. Inscribed on the floor, in front of the statue are the words: 'That Whitsun I was late getting away – Philip Larkin Poet & Librarian 1922-1985'

All the seating in the lobby was now occupied. There was a steady stream of comings and goings from the low-key station doorway to the more magnificent York stone entrance off Ferensway.

'Hull has a vibrant, if not colourful history,' I began. 'How does it compare to other cities when it comes to ghosts and hauntings. Some sceptics might -'

'It's much the same as any other city,' said Mike, cutting in. 'Take Ye Olde White Harte, for example. It's said to be haunted by those who conspired there to bar King Charles I from entering Hull in 1642, an edict that was said to have led to the outbreak of the English civil War. In my experience once you've done one haunted pub, you've done them all. As a parapsychologist you have to be willing to branch out and look at a variety of different locations. As for the so-called "sceptics", the word seemed to drip of his tongue as he spat it out. 'One thing that annoys me more than the credulity of someone willing to believe anything they hear on the topic of ghosts, is the dogmatic sceptic, who refuses point blank to consider the possibility of their existence. Surely,' he added a little more reflectively, 'wouldn't you'd prefer the company of someone who seeks the truth, than someone who thinks they have found it?'

A loud bang echoed above our heads, followed by heavy footsteps. Dressed in a cream bathrobe and wearing a pair of open-toed, white slippers a heavily-set man appeared at the top of the former Victorian staircase (restored after a fire in 1990). Fist clenched and arms flailing he strode down the stairs, marched purposely through the lobby and slammed what looked like a broken tap onto the reception desk.

The young girl in attendance smiled weakly at the man. Words were exchanged. Apologies made. The man was handed a different set of keys and shown to his new room by the porter.

'And there,' said Mike, his mood brightening, 'Is one apparition I can explain away.' He drained what was left of his coffee and excused himself.

About ten minutes went by while Mike went to the toilets, during which I learned a lot about the origins of the tradition of afternoon tea from the menu on our table:

In the 19th century, and according to legend (it read on the inside cover), one of Queen Victoria's ladies-in-waiting, Anna Marie Stanhope (1783-1857), known as the Duchess of Bedford, was credited for creating afternoon tea. The noon meal she had been given had become skimpier and the Duchess had suffered from 'a sinking feeling' at about four o'clock in the afternoon. At first, she had her servants sneak her a pot of tea and a few breadstuffs. Adopting the European tea service format, she soon invited friends to join her in what became an additional afternoon meal at five o'clock in her rooms at Belvoir Castle...

'Much of the hotel's paranormal activity, or "hotspots", as we call them,' said Mike on his return, 'have occurred at two separate locations at either end of the third floor. We'll setup the recording equipment at the far end of the west wing, to begin with,' he continued, picking up his backpack. 'Whilst it's running we'll make our way to the front of the hotel, on the east. Do a few tests there, before returning to the original site.' Direct in approach there was an almost military-style precision to Mike's well-thought-out plans.

As we reached the third floor landing it was clear that much of the hotel's Victorian character had been carefully preserved. There were; restful wallpaper, of yellow and soft pinks; high domed ceilings, flourished with white rose carvings; flickering wall lights, reminiscent of the smaller Rochester brass fittings; intricately carved wood panelling and corridors with names such as; Georgian, Sandringham, Victorian, Empire, Humber and York. It was this wilful attention to detail that set the hotel apart from others in the city.

Mike pushed open the doors that led to the Prince Albert Suite, 'In you go,' he said, ushering me inside with an after-you herding gesture. Hitching the backpack higher onto his right shoulder he followed closely behind.

Where there would normally be six to ten people on any one investigation (the group awash with talk of supernatural experiences and nervous laughter), there were two of us. Feeling a little nervous and exposed - falling only slightly short of an honest-to-goodness panic with the prospect of coming up against some otherworldly manifestation for the first time - I walked with some uncertainty down the first of many dimly lit corridors.

The further we went the more our surroundings became blander, austere even. The corridors were gloomy and cold. Cracks appeared on the walls and a strong musty smell hung in the air like stale, wet mildew. It was the kind of smell you sensed with your teeth and wrapped itself around your tongue. For want of a better analogy, a scene from a Gothic Melodrama came to mind.

'This should do,' said Mike, coming to a stop.

We had reached the furthest most part of the west wing. On the far right there was a storeroom. Its door was painted dark green and chipped. And directly ahead, a wood panelled window overlooked the station.

Looking down the view seemed somewhat disjointed, almost as if it had been modelled on a child's view of the railway station, a model which refused to be constrained by imagination. The concourse and five bay trainshed looked to be moulded from tainted plasticine and crumpled silver and grey toffee-wrappers, glued to half-licked lollipop sticks.

'The thing about investigations in my field -' said Mike, conversationally, (he seemed animated beneath the iridescent light, I noticed, as he busied himself with unpacking the recording equipment,) 'is it's like a game of snakes and ladders. Just when you make what looks like a breakthrough you suddenly hit a brick wall and back down you go again.'

Silent for a moment he took a few digital photographs and performed base line tests to ascertain any areas of EMF activity; creaking floorboards and the location of power lines and power points that might interfere with the recordings. The EMF, he had earlier explained, was used to detect any Electro Magnetic Fields, or as he put it: 'The presence of any non-human activity or strange phenomena.' One EMF was placed beneath the window and a second outside the storeroom.

A small trellis table was set up in the middle of the corridor and a silver cross placed on a white piece of paper. A black line was drawn around the cross, tracing the outline to show any movement. A video camera was placed on a tripod facing the table – also a good area around which to show any interference.

'There, that should do it,' said Mike, taking a step back and inspecting his display, somewhat like and hard-to-please artist.

'Will the equipment be safe here?'

'What?' he said distractedly. 'Oh, yes. This is the quietest part of the hotel. There are no guest rooms, as you can see and besides, this is where -' pausing theatrically for a moment, his eyes flashed towards me, as if inviting a response, '- there have been sightings of a small child,' he continued. 'She, we think she's a girl,' he quickly added, 'has been seen wandering the corridor, before disappearing through the window.'

Finally a dictaphone was set to record outside the store room. This was done to perform an EVP (Electro Voice Phenomena), Mike explained, to see if we could pick up on the tape any voices or noises that couldn't be explained by people being in the building or by any background noise.

'Oh, by the way,' he said with a wry smile. 'If you see any strange shadows, let me know. We think there might be a second spirit wandering around up here.'

Sometimes it was hard to know if Mike was being serious. At times his smile would fade and become a grin of childlike duplicity. But this time his face betrayed no hint of amusement as he picked up the backpack.

'Come on,' he said, heading back down the corridor. 'Let's go.'
'Where to?' In no hurry to stay, I followed on closely behind.
'The other side of the hotel, of course…'

The Victorian Suite on the east wing was much busier and brighter than the Prince Albert. Many of the rooms were occupied. The corridors were vibrant and awash with the sound of muffled TVs and, if you listened carefully, the remnants of other peoples' conversations. Two men passed us. They were heading in the opposite direction. The taller one I noticed had a pot-marked face. His hair was black and tied back in a pony tail, like a free-trade market seller. Smartly dressed in a light grey suit, his companion was younger and walked with a pronounced limp, which accentuated every other step.

'Have you ever seen a ghost wearing the top hat?' said Mike as he came to a stop at the end of the corridor.

Not knowing what to say, I shook my head.

'Well, this is where one has been seen.' He opened his arms wide, like a ringmaster introducing a new act. 'What's interesting about this apparition,' he continued eagerly, 'is that he appears to turn towards the viewer and smile, before disappearing.'

Nervously backing towards the wall, I checked for the nearest exit… Just in case. There was something distinctly unnerving about a ghost that seemed aware of its surroundings.

Using a digital thermometer Mike took a number of readings up and down the corridor. Apart from a slight drop in the ambient temperature there was little to record. Several more experiments were conducted using equipment similar to the EMF and EVP machines, but no unusual phenomenon was detected.

'Unfortunately,' said Mike after a while, 'it's not always possible to record something of interest.' There was more than a hint of disappointment in his voice. 'We might as well go back and check the recordings.'

There was a quietness between us that seemed sharp and drawn out as we retraced our steps back through the hotel's corridors. The air grew colder and the cracks appeared once more, giving a real sense of the past returning.

To our surprise (mine more than Mike's) when we got back, the cross on the table seemed to have moved a small amount. It appeared to have rotated about 3mm around its centre, the bottom of the cross moving to the right. When we reviewed the video we were unable to make out any movement.

Puzzled at first Mike's face suddenly broke into a wide grin. 'Maybe there's an alternative explanation,' he laughed. 'What if the cross was moved slowly over the entire period of the experiment making it almost impossible to see?'

'Is that relevant?'

'It means that if we run the video through the tracking software on the computer, there's a chance we might... just might pick something up not visible to the naked eye.' His grin widened some more.

There were also a number of orbs on the video recording (believed by many to be ghosts in the form of light balls) but this, as Mike explained, could have easily been put down to the movement of dust particles after we had disturbed the floor.

Although several background noises could be heard on the dictaphone - the slow screeching from passenger trains and the garbled sound of the station tannoy announcing the arrival of the 22:44 from Manchester Piccadilly - two noises remained unexplained. One sounded somewhat like a chair being dragged across a concrete floor (the hotel's floor was carpeted). And the other what could have been a child's giggle.

The interesting thing was that the video recording showed no one coming and going while we were away. Mike replayed the audio tape several times and conceded that he couldn't make sense of the two unusual sounds. 'I'll get the tape cleaned up tomorrow,' he said. 'Removing the background noises might help make things clearer.'

He took the digital tape from the dictaphone and placed it into a clear plastic bag.

Checking his wristwatch, Mike turned towards me and shrugged. 'Time's getting on,' he said. 'I think we should call it a night. Besides,' he quickly added, as if handing out a runners-up prize. 'We'll probably come back in the New Year to do a more thorough investigation. You're welcome to join me and the rest of the Ghost Chasers team, if you want?'

When we reached the ground floor the lobby was deserted. The bar was shuttered for the night and the tubular lights dimmed to a soft glow, like the embers of a dying fire. As we shook hands and we went our separate ways Mike promised to email me the results of the audio and video analysis, as soon as he had them.

It was raining hard as I left the hotel. The air was cold and sweet with the smell of the nearby takeaways. Music boomed from the Tower night club. Headlights from passing cars flashed in the heavy rain, momentarily blurring the boundaries between the light and the dark. A metaphor, perhaps (we humans like to think in such images), for a bridge of light between the living and the dead - a continuity, albeit of a spectral kind.

While it was all too easy to get caught up in the drama of the investigation, the question still remained: was there enough evidence to support the hypothesis that the hotel was haunted?

As my taxi pulled away from the hotel's car park, I had to concede that, in the cold light of day (at one in the morning first light wasn't too far away), without any verifiable scientific proof, the answer would be no. However, given the true nature of any paranormal evidence (subjective or otherwise), there would always be enough to warrant further investigations into what, in essence, is a self-perpetuating search for the truth.

With this in mind, perhaps I might ... just might take Mike Smith up on his offer and return in the New Year.

Foundations

Kate Cooper

Unlike many places, whose boundaries have barely changed since 1066, there is no mention of Hull in the Domesday Book. There may have been a small settlement near the river mouth, and there was a ferry from Grimsby that crossed the Humber somewhere near, but no more. Hull grew in size as it grew in prosperity, and that, as so often throughout the centuries, was down to immigration.

In the early 12th century a small group of monks left their monastery on the Ile-de-France and sailed to the north coast of England, where they were granted land by the Bishop of York in his jurisdiction of Beverley. Like immigrants the world over, they named the abbey they established there in memory of their home, Meaux. The abbey quickly grew in size and importance, predominantly based in their trade in wool. They needed a port from which to export the wool, which fetched huge prices on the continent, and settled on Hull. Within two hundred years Hull had grown to a substantial port. By now, not only was it exporting £4000 of wool a year, but was importing timber, French wine and Burgundy cider in vast amounts.

Imagine we are in Hull in 1300. What, if anything, will we recognise? Can we catch a glimpse of the Medieval town? We are talking of a much smaller town than you might think; far smaller than what we now call The Old Town, which expanded later in the 14th century, but which in 1300 was contained in an area that ran, in today's terms, up the length of Queen's Gardens and along until it met the River Hull at Drypool, south down High Street to Scale Lane, and then west, passing along Silver Street and Whitefriargate, to complete its circuit.

If you can fix that area in your mind's eye, you're probably surprised to find Holy Trinity outside the boundary. But don't worry, in 1300 you will see it rising magnificently over the town as you expect, but beyond the walls, and soon enough it will be engulfed by the increasing populace. It was founded as a chapelry, a kind of satellite church, to stop parishioners having to trudge all the way to their mother church at Hessle, but the riches the town is now enjoying enabled the Corporation of the town to build a permanent place of worship. They hoped to emulate Beverley, but the Hull of this time was so much smaller than its more famous neighbour, they had to set their sights a little lower.

In Lowgate, however, you will find the real church of old Hull, St. Mary's. It too was established as a chapelry, its mother church at Ferriby in the diocese of Drypool. In 1300 it remained so, but within twenty years the foundations will be laid for a church that in its time will be bigger than Holy Trinity. (And will remain so until a certain Tudor king decides to demolish most of it as it obscures the view of the river from his house in the town.)

St. Mary's is named for St. Mary Magdalene, whose feast day is on May 25th. So, as is common everywhere, that's when the annual fair comes to Hull, one of the earliest and longest in the country. In 1279 the charter was first issued for a market and fair, and seven acres set aside for them. There are markets here twice a week and villagers from the neighbourhood come in to buy and sell basic goods, but the fair is the chance to pick up more exotic imports; figs, oranges, pomegranates, spices, dyes, and to find the latest fashions and textiles. People will be keeping a lookout this year for the new blue fabrics, only just obtainable, and only for the very rich. There is no dyeing industry here, so the wool Hull exports is dyed in Flanders and sent back for the English mercers to weave.

The fair attracts thousands of visitors, far outnumbering the local population, and they come in all sorts. Rich merchants trading wholesale, whose laden hulks lay offshore; tradesmen out to part people from their money by hook or by crook; mummers and guisers who set up stalls to entertain an audience avid for entertainment; beggars and, cliché though it is, thieves. A man needs to have his wits about him at Hull fair.

Hull apprentices are given a day off at the beginning of the fair by their masters, and roam the streets in gangs, getting drunk and making a nuisance of themselves. One of their regular scams is to pick on strangers, easily identified by their speech or clothes, and make their lives a misery. They used to love taunting the Jews when they were here, throwing stones at their conical hats, just asking to be knocked off, but it's been ten years since the King got rid of the lot of them.

We haven't mentioned Edward I yet, have we? He's been the real making of the town, quite literally. For the past seven years it has proudly borne the name of Kingstown upon Hull, and because he values it so highly, money has been flowing even more. He garrisons his army here for the Scottish campaigns, and soldiers are often seen about the town, spending money. (Much of it, as you might guess, on drink and prostitutes. In fact, it's common practice for prostitutes to pay the garrison rent to use the walls for their trade.)

Just this year the King has built an Exchange Hall and a Mint that produces silver pennies. There's talk of an Assay office. He's opened up trade as well. Old Wyke was very selective in whom it dealt with, but now traders come from far afield; not only Flanders but all the towns of the Hanseatic League and many from the Italian states. Indeed the Frescobaldis from Lucca and Bardis from Florence have been coming here so long they have tenancies in the town.

Mind you, they pay heavily for the privilege. The town bailiffs set the taxes and charge more to outsiders by far. They ban the import or export of wool altogether, to protect local jobs, and only a year or so back seized forty bags from a Pontefract man and sank a Flanders vessel out at sea. Men from Scarborough aren't allowed to trade here at all. But you'll certainly hear a huge variety of tongues and dialects on the streets.

Writing *Hull*

The building going on throughout the town has needed carpenters and masons to swell the local tradesmen, and you may be surprised to see how often they use brick, instead of timber or stone. That's because brickmaking is a major industry here. In fact this year, 1300, it is second only to London in the numbers it produces. For now, only ten cities in the country have more brick buildings than Hull.

Possibly the greatest difference you will notice among the people of 1300 Hull from today is the amount of clergy about the town. Throughout the country, spiritual life was a crucial ingredient to everyday living and clerics of all kinds are visible wherever you go. The abbots from Meaux, though they sold their land to the King, are still often in town negotiating trade deals and overseeing their other businesses. The Carmelite Friars have a house on Aldgate, where they have set up a small hospital for the poor. They can often be seen about the town in their distinctive white scapulars, spreading their ministry. The Austin friars are further out, towards the river, but they too are clearly recognisable by their black habits. They are all well thought of in the town, and will be remembered centuries after they have vanished in streets named for them.

The docks themselves, on the River Hull, are noisy and busy, jammed with every kind of vessel from the trading hulks to wherries, arsenal ships to barges. The King sent out an order to dig out latrines near here, to ease the foul smell in the town, but nobody bothers much. The aldermen and guildsmen, who would pay for them, as taxpayers, think it would be far too costly an undertaking.

These men, and the wealthier burghers, are very concerned about money, and lay down strict rules about punishments to those caught offending, but surprisingly, Hull has no stocks, as most other towns do. Money is set aside, though, to pay for guards to check wagons and carts coming into, and going out of, the town through Mytongate or Aldgate. They're mainly checking for smuggled goods coming in, and felons trying to escape going out. Any criminal, even a murderer, will be deemed free if he reaches sanctuary and stays there long enough. If he gets as far as Beverley, he is free immediately.

In 1300 Hull is a prosperous, fast expanding town. And for the next few decades, as it grows up around the Market Place and out towards Wincolmlee, it seems as if its fortunes will only continue to improve in this fashion. But in 1300, neither Hull, nor anyone else in Europe, could foresee 1349 and the horrors of the Black Death.

Writing *Hull*

What are Boyes made of?

Alison Wood

How does Father Christmas come to your home? A traditional slide down a sooty chimney, legs kicking at the flames? Or has your absent stack and central heating forced magic keys to be cut for that one night? In Scarborough he comes early. In Scarborough he comes by sea and here I am to welcome this beaming, beardy, benefactor.

It's sunny with brushes of cloud and a breeze teases my ears telling me winter is here. It's a get-your-gloves-on day. Hummanby Silver Band sport Santa hats with Remembrance Day poppies pinned on. Is it really only six weeks away? I feel like I've only just taken last year's decorations down. The band members blow Christmas carols through lips young and old. A festive feeling floats along the harbour side.

'When's he coming?' a lady asks me.

'Eleven o' clock,' I reply. 'And it's not like him to be late.' I peer at her watch.

'Plenty time,' I say but we both still strain our eyes to the far entrance of the triangular, walled harbour, to scout his whereabouts. The pavement is now thick with folks, dogs, pushchairs and a tin man, a witch, a lion and a Dorothy.

'There's a scarecrow over there!' A beside-himself boy points and true enough all straw and rags, a scarecrow squeezes past.

A thousand people now frame the harbour and spill up Eastborough toward the town centre. And who makes this possible? I know but for those who don't, look down and read the name on the side of the big plastic bag a lad in lederhosen has just thrust at me, take a free sweet or two and look again. Boyes. Boyes for good value. Boyes - our town's family run business since 1881. I know you want to see Santa, but wait, I want to tell you about this extraordinary company that is part of mine, and Hull's, shopping landscape.

Victorian spa town Scarborough had a thriving fishing industry and was well connected by rail to transport fish out and transport tourists in. A working class community wanted clothes to match their budgets. With his own funding and using the wit of youth Scarborian William Boyes drew on his drapery apprenticeship in London and the Midlands and the contacts he had made there and brought his intentions home. At twenty-two he opened a small store in Eastborough, 'The Remnant Warehouse', selling odd lots and end pieces from merchants. Stitching clothes from this bargain cloth made fine affordable attire and news travelled as fast as the housewives could sew.

'You can make a dress cheaper than anywhere else in town! And a coat! Go to Boyes!'

And they did. A mere fourteen feet of counter space did not stop locals visiting 'The Rem' as it became fondly known. In 1885, as William bought in clearance lines from more sellers, he had to move to larger premises on Market Street. World fairs were diminishing as consumers demanded variety and proximate purchasing. The Remnant Warehouse transformed into a department store and counter upon counter unfurled, until in 1892, three floors were filled. The Scarborough Mercury devoted an article congratulating William on having "an emporium no economical housewife can afford to ignore."

Voltaic William produced on-site electricity and strutted six hundred feet of counter space by 1896. He kept his office in the store and personally did all the buying and checking of goods, while his forty assistants tended the convergence of customers. The Evening News described it as "one of the most complete and convenient business premises in Yorkshire."

On my quest to explore Boyes' continued expansion towards Hull I visited the store in Bridlington. After taking the stairs, though a lift is always available, to the third floor I browse past the Boyes Home

Chutneys and into the small museum. It is delightful, arranged as the Victorian store, with a wide counter and pictures, newspaper cuttings and merchandise encased on the walls. Costume clad mannequins welcome the customer. The theme runs into the adjoining bay café, where waitresses in frilly maid's hats repeat ready orders, while the diner's attention is somewhere at sea.

A little girl drags her bag-laden Grandmother in.

'Oh sweetheart not again! We've been in here a hundred times!' she pants.

'I know,' says the catalogue model child, her perfect blue eyes alight. 'But I love it.'

Her Grandmother turns to me. 'I've been buying cloth here all my life. There's nothing you can't get here, it's good for, well...'

'Everything?' I offer.

'Yes, everything.' She bustles off, her excited granddaughter making her forget her heavy load.

Because I consider I know William a little by now, I feel a moment of pride as I meet him in sepia on the wall and discover his sons, George and Robert, followed him into the business. There is no doubt they worked hard. The J.C. King High Class Ledgers, laid on the counter, show the hundreds of independent businesses Boyes traded with. Communications today would make sourcing goods a time consuming but easier task. Imagine doing the same in 1889. I notice they have been buying from Cussons at least since the 1960s. I wonder if the soap makers are still a family run business.

The beginning of the twentieth century saw William seek extra capital and he formed William Boyes and Company Limited, with himself as managing director. Extra funding allowed for further expansion. Properties on the adjoining Queen's Street were bought and demolished and a new building constructed, in 1901, with an elegant frontage linking Queen's Street with the Market Street store at a right angle to appear as one shop. Flags flew from the four towers of this stately forty thousand square foot concern. The corner octagonal tower held four clock faces, crafted by the family founded firm Potts of Leeds, who are still in business today and designed by Edmund Beckett Denison (Lord Grimthorpe), who also created the world famous Palace of Westminster clock, known commonly as Big Ben. Each clock was electrically lit by night, throwing out time over the town to remind prospective patrons when it was the waking moment not to miss a Boyes bargain.

'Mum! What's that? Mum, I'm scared! It's doing it again!' A child's shrieks compete with the drumming of shells sent from Admiral Franz von Hipper's battleships. His mother flies to the window of their shivering quayside cottage.

'It's all right love, leave your breakfast and get your sister, quick. I'll grab the little ones. We need to go and see your aunty up town. Don't cry sweetie, it'll be fine. Go on, hurry!'

German naval intelligence had shown Scarborough to have little military defence, an open shipping lane and a mineless sea. On the sixteenth of December, in the first few months of the Great War, for ninety monstrous, measureless minutes the raid on the town blasted the prominent Grand Hotel, churches and homes. One hundred and thirty seven lives were taken and nearly six hundred people were injured, many of them civilians. The public raged at the enemy attack and the neglect of the navy to safekeep Scarborough. This provoked a war commission to artist E. Kemp-Welsh, who produced a propaganda poster, in 1915, showing Britannia brandishing the British flag, leading citizens from a pastoral landscape towards the port, where a fury of flames rage behind St. Mary's church and onto the skyline. The message, 'Remember Scarborough! Enlist Now.'

The store survived the blitz, but it wasn't all plain sailing for the seaside Boyes and Sons. On February 26th, 1915 the Scarborough Pictorial printed a souvenir issue and claimed the disaster that struck the department store as 'The biggest fire in the town's history.' The blaze reduced 'The Rem' to 'matchwood.' Seventy thousand pounds of damage in two hours. The equivalent of approximately four million pounds today. The neighbouring Queen's Street Chapel was also gutted in the inferno. I met with Andrew Boyes, Managing Director, to interview him on several aspects of the company and asked him what he knew of the fire. He smiled.

'We blame it on the chapel and the chapel blame it on us. But we did have some gas lighting on the premises, so it was likely down to those.' William, Andrew's great-grandfather, had been away on a business trip, returning to departmental devastation. Although not in good health, but with character intact, William swiftly rented alternative trading premises and began organising reconstruction of the scorched site. With World War One fighting spirit Boyes rebuilt a smart Queen's Street store, opening in 1916, less that seventeen months after the fire. It still stands today. Was the fire a good thing? I had asked Andrew Boyes. He answered, 'The only fortunate thing about the fire was that it happened in the night and no one was there.'

So what hunk of this history occupies Hull? Let's hop aboard an ocean liner, an autobus or even zip over in a Zeppelin and behold.

Boyes traded in Prospect Street, Hull for a short time just after the limited company was formed. The lease was sold on after a couple of years, in 1901. Hull had to wait until 1920 when a draper sold his shop on 232 to 234 Hessle Road, corner Constable Street. A newspaper advert announced a takeover sale, a sale so spectacular the store had to close for a day to prepare. I peer at the page and feel a flapping 20s February.

'W Boyes and Co beg to announce they have purchased the well known business of Mr J Wardell. Mr W Boyes commenced business in a very small way 38 years ago and we now have two large stores in Scarborough and York where 'Boyes' has become a household name. The main features of our business are

1.Anyone is at perfect liberty to walk around without being under the slightest obligation to purchase.

2. We will gladly refund the money or exchange the goods for any purchase which does not give your entire satisfaction.

3. We are large buyers of 'Manufacturers' stocks and clearance, bankrupt and salvage stocks and you can always be sure of the BEST VALUE OBTAINABLE.'

There is still a sale at Boyes on the same date as this every year but I was curious to discover if these business features had changed over the years. My meeting with Andrew Boyes gave me a privileged insight into the family business. There's no email hot line to the nerve centre of Boyes, unless you are a supplier, so I wrote to request an interview. I received a very enthusiastic electronic reply and Mr Boyes offered to meet me at the head office in Eastfield, just outside Scarborough. The offices had been moved from the Scarborough store in the seventies, allowing more space for the café to flourish and to seek a site to build a stock warehouse.

Andrew Boyes has a hand shake as warm as his summer sky eyes. He looks in his middle years, though it seemed impolite to ask and modern media is too preoccupied with age, that I make a mindful manoeuvre to disregard it. His suit was smart and the tones of his tie harmonised in an untroubled way and I felt very comfortable sat with him at the end of the yawning oak boardroom table.

So what does drive a family run business in 2010?

He answered sincerely by telling me that the principles his great-grandfather had, still hold today. Value, variety and service. The business runs on repeat selling. Because customers don't spend a lot each visit, it is important that they come back. One of the fundamental bases of ensuring this happens in retail, is customer service. Andrew feels it is a forgotten art, but not in his shops, where staff are valued and seen as part of the 'family team.'

'You're only as good as the worst member of staff on a bad day,' he confides. 'So if a young girl has had an argument with her boyfriend the night before, then it could be a hard day.'

Boyes staff are trained to help the customers, be friendly and smile. The company are keen to retain their staff. I do recognise most of the staff in my local store.

And prices?

'It's not about the cheapest product,' Andrew tells me. 'It's about the best value product at the right price.'

I recounted my visit to the Bridlington museum and my flipping through the ledger's lists of all the suppliers. He sighed and told me regrettably it's not like that anymore. The market is not UK led, technology has brought more global trading and the big brands manufacture overseas. Yet Boyes want to keep up with the modern shopper, meet their needs and offer something different.

I asked him about the store layout, I have visited several now and they have very similar interiors.

Is it intentional?

'Yes it is.' He nods. 'We want the same feel, even though the shopping experience is constantly evolving.'

What makes it different?

'Craft, haberdashery, material and wool,' Is his swift reply. 'It's a trade we know and are good at, so was easy to keep.' I told him my wedding tiara was made from materials from his haberdashery department and it's amazing.

'Really? Oh, good for you!' he laughs.

Andrew continued to explain how important the heritage of the company is to him, that it feels like being a trustee. This ancestry can be built on. Andrew sees a family business to have an alternative mindset to newer companies, some of which he considers to be in for short term gains. Boyes focus on long term ventures. They have not partaken in today's debt culture, fast expansion and sell out quick. Boyes do not carry debt and they pay their suppliers on time.

Are there any other secrets to success?

Andrew doesn't require time to think. 'Know every manager in every shop,' he discloses. 'Visit them as often as you can, keep your ears to the ground and interact with the customers.'

So is being part of the institution inbred or expected?

'Absolutely not,' Andrew states emphatically. 'There was no pressure to join the business, emotionally or otherwise.'

When he decided it was his vocation Andrew completed one of the first business degrees, nationally, in Manchester. I imagined him in his springtime as he spoke and decided he would have been an all-absorbing initiate, he has a little star in his eye. His son, fifth generation of the founder William, was allowed the same surrender and also chose to join the company, bringing an invaluable business and information technology degree with him. This is telling. The family could keep learning in-house and rest on success but they get out there and put their backs into what else is happening in the trade. There is management moving and shaking behind those shop fronts.

I asked Andrew to take a trip back with me to 1920s Hull and he promptly climbed aboard. 'Oh we are very fond of our Hull stores.' He glowed. 'After all they were part of our early expansion.'

Hessle Road, then, was in the midst of the fervent fishing trade. The shop opened long hours to try and catch a bit of the bounty generated by those salty seams. Fishermen worked hard, played hard, mostly in the Criterion pub near the shop, then tipped the remaining pence up to their lasses to run the home. Fortunately some was spent in Boyes and steadily over the years, after surviving World War Two raids, adjoining shops and land were bought up, added and built upon to make the store that stands today. For many years the Hessle Road store roof banner named it 'Boyes Walk Round Store' encouraging browsing for bargains. Painted between the windows were elephants and sale standards exclaiming 'Don't be surprised if Boyes have elephants for a penny each!' In the 1960s elephants did stroll up Hessle Road, wearing tabards telling 'We're off to Boyes' and 'Are there really elephants at Boyes?' I was told they were not for sale. A relief, fitting them into the boot of a 1960s Mini could have been tricky.

What did fit into the sixties was the Boyes venture into the vibrant suburb around Holderness Road in Hull. The chosen site originally, in the early 1900s, hosted costumiers and milliners, then a joiners. When the movies went talky and entertainment was an affordable pastime for many, a super cinema, The Savoy Picture Theatre, was developed there. As the film industry boomed The Savoy was reconstructed in 1937, with good wishes for the opening night coming from, among others, Laurence Olivier and Vivienne Leigh.

The decades watched the cinemas decline. In the 1960s, possibly due to television and change in leisure tastes, many closed, including The Savoy. Fine Fare foods grabbed the lease and Boyes took it over in 1965. By 1970 the Hessle and Holderness Roads combined reached sales of one million pounds.

For the Hull hat-trick Boyes were one of the first businesses to sign up for a space in the new Bransholme Shopping Centre in 1973, now a larger complex known as North Point Shopping Centre. Hull City Council developed Bransholme estate to house the city's overspill population. Andrew Boyes commented on how pleased they were to secure this site. The estate houses approximately fifty thousand people; most of the families who moved there in the seventies were from around the Hessle Road area and keen Boyes shoppers. Andrew Boyes stated, 'We felt like we were taking our customers with us.'

And they did. The centre is still busy with budget stores, yet Boyes still offer that family-fangled twist that sets them apart.

I informed a delighted Andrew that the larger-than-life bronze statue of the poet Philip Larkin had hidden outside the Paragon Station concourse in Hull, under metres of cloth provided by Boyes, awaiting the Lord Mayor to uncover it as a lasting legacy to Larkin's connection to Hull.

Were there any Hull anecdotes Andrew could share with me?

He pointed to an elegant winged trophy Boyes had won and expresses his thanks to a creative young man they had hired for a radio advertising campaign aimed at Hull residents. Apparently the young man went into the Boyes stores in Hull and offered to pay for the goods in shopper's baskets if they could tell him the name of the shop. Easy, they all replied 'Boysies!'

Does it bother Andrew that the name is pronounced wrongly?

'Not at all,' Andrew chuckles. 'We're included in *Learn to Speak 'Ull*. In Beverley we are known as Boyez,' he pronounces in a ritzy accent and we both smile.

Bob Boyes managed Hessle Road for a great many years and was known for buying in very odd lots, including all the cabin fittings and linen from a passing boat being taken out of service. Bob also liked to stand in for the Father Christmas in the Grotto. One year he was staging Santa antics in the shop front window and the passing traffic stopped to watch. The police didn't take kindly to the Hessle Road halting and went in to speak to the manager, who of course popped over to speak to them in a red suit and a long white beard. Ho, ho, ho.

Christmas has always been a special feature in the company. A Scarborough newspaper advert in 1927 for Boyes Christmas bazaar encouraged inhabitants to: 'Visit Boyes Christmas attraction! A trip to the moon by aeroplane. Never before has such a stupendous and realistic attraction been placed before the public of the district. Tickets for the journey are handed to each passenger by Father Christmas himself. Entrancing scenic effects of a Pixie Waterfall, Aladdin's cave and lamp, the naughty boy Peter Pan, the Wishing Bridge, Father Christmas in his workshop, the dream ship, polar bears...'

And so it went on. How wonderful to be in 'The Store Between the Bays' and experience how breathtaking an encounter with the moon would be. I could have worn my economy fashion Boyes gay waterproof for the dull days, with its detachable hood, narrow tie belt and jetted pockets, just the thing for holiday packing and a Pixie Waterfall.

Why does the company continue with the lavish grotto and the Christmas window display each year at the Scarborough store? It's rather Hamleys and they don't have to do it these days.

'I know we don't have to do it,' Andrew explains. 'But we'd be in trouble if we didn't.' He laughs. It's something that stores did and Boyes chose to carry it on. People expect it and it's goodwill for the company brand.

'We don't let the accountants loose on it,' he continues. 'It doesn't make any money!'

A valued staff member has been creating the themes for a number of years now and enjoys doing it. I visited the grotto this year, after witnessing staff still painting it at closing time the night before it opened. I met life sized Wizard of Oz characters, a spinning house and a girl calling for home, though I stopped at sitting on Santa's lap, a tad beyond the call of research. It creates a real buzz in the store and the children love it. Andrew feels it gives something back to the community.

Boyes contribute to the community in many ways. They have sponsored the yachting North Sea Race and a day at Scarborough Cricket Festival each year. They give money to school sports, Saint Catherine's Hospice and donate prizes for raffles at charity events. But something that Andrew is very proud of and his heart swelled through his suit jacket when he told me, is the local EASY bands they support. Eastern Area Schools Youth bands. For twenty eight years Boyes involvement has brought Scarborough school's musical youth firmly on to the melodious map. Consequently the bands have done extremely well in national competitions and Boyes sponsor an annual celebrity concert at The Spa, Scarborough, where a big name in jazz is invited to come and perform with the bands to reward and inspire them.

So, I query, will Boyes be hosting a Junior Apprentice? The boardroom is ready and waiting.

'Oh, no.' Andrew grins. 'But if I did I wouldn't send them on such grand challenges. You can send a young person to Whitby with no money and ask them to make it back. That would show their initiative!'

From one shop to forty shops. From one county to seven. From a few remnants to thirty thousand different products. From a hand cart to a sixteen tonne lorry. From a cheeky monkey Jacko who lived with his friends on the top floor of the Scarborough store, to the unveiling, by the Queen of a statue 'The Family' to embody the values and aims of Boyes and their principles that earned them an invitation to be part of the Billingham retail complex. From William becoming Mayor of Scarborough to the fifth generation still working hard in The Rem. From a trip to the moon to a trip to Oz. I thanked this gentleman, Andrew Boyes, for sharing moments in this dealing dynasty and he wished me well with my writing.

'He's here!' A tiny girl with a victorious vantage point on her father's shoulders points and then flaps her arms like a humming bird.

'Where did he come from?' I exclaim, having looked away from the harbour mouth for only a second.

'The North Pole?' somebody offers.

Well I'm impressed. In glides Skylark, a small local fishing boat, like one a child would draw, half the hull painted in a thick stripe of blue and above it sunflower yellow. Its fluorescent orange buoys dangle over the sides like huge Christmas baubles. And here he is, on cue to 'Santa Claus is coming to town,' waving at his fluttering crowd.

The Witch of the West shows she is not so wicked and holds out a hand to steady him off the boat. Father Christmas, salutary slender this year, smoulders through the swarm, smiling, shaking teensy hands and jabbering with his tizzied audience. A nugget of emotion fills my throat and my eyelids tingle. Boyes succeed in giving back. Santa slings himself up on the Christmas float and signals so-long for now, as he motors off up Eastborough, to settle in his grotto.

I wend my way up the cobbles to my home and spot a neighbour.

'Hello,' I greet him. 'I've just been down the seafront to watch Santa arrive!' I'm still a little excited and want everyone to have a part in it.

'So, he's here then?' He shines. 'I must tell the kids!' Though in his sixties, one can no longer judge the age people chose to become parents.

'Aw, how old are they?' I ask.

'Forty two and forty four,' he replies. 'But they still like to know he's here.'

So there may be little boy(e)s in all of us.

Writing *Hull*

Quilting the Light Fantastic

Kate Cooper

Somewhere at home, I have an old photograph of my parents and me, taken at a dance, in the days when eleven year olds didn't squirm with embarrassment at the thought of spending an evening out with the family. I could probably find it if I had to, but I don't need it to picture it clearly. I'm wearing a blue dress that has long since vanished, but Mum is wearing a glorious 1960s brocade cocktail dress, with rich red flowers woven in circles on a glossy black ground, the bodice tight and the skirt wide, showing her impossibly narrow waist. I've put a patch of that fabric, a complete, shimmering circle, right in the middle of the quilt I've made for her.

I can't remember how young I was when I first went to stay for the night at my granny's, with my cousin, while our parents went out to a dinner-dance. The Work's 'do', the Remembrance Day Ball, the local Silver Band's annual fundraiser. But I do remember the swish and the colours of the wonderful frocks, new every time, and how I thought my mother looked like a queen. (When I was a bit older, and had seen pictures, I thought she looked like the Queen.) Ted the taxi man would drive them off, and when we children woke up next morning, there would be balloons inexplicably bouncing round the living room for us, and always boxes of chocolates or sweets; my Dad was great at all the spot prizes. "Who's got a wooden door key?" "First man here with a pair of stockings over his arm." "Bring me a portrait of the Queen."

When I was about five, the dress was luscious dark pink grosgrain with a shawl collar and a side pleat in the skirt caught up into a rose on the hip. I wish I'd kept that rose, but a rescued patch of the stiff fabric with its subtle sheen sits perfectly in the corner of the quilt. I was too young to have ever seen them dance together then, but I could picture Mum in that pink, swirling round the floor, her small feet in gunmetal leather stilettos gliding effortlessly, and Dad in one of his much-loved suits, while a big band played. I knew they'd met at a dance, and went dancing every night until just before I was born. I thought everybody's parents did.

I'm not sure now when I first went with them, but I think I must have been about nine. The family was together as usual; parents, two sets of aunts and uncles, four cousins. The band played up on a high stage, there were tables set four deep around three sides of the room and, between the two, a huge expanse of gleaming parquet. When we looked up we could see hundreds of balloons caught up in nets at the ceiling, ready to cascade down at the end of the night, and one little mystery was solved. When the music started, Mum and Dad were among the first up, not because they were extroverts, (in fact they were rather shy, I now realise,) but simply because they loved to glide round that floor, happy to enjoy the moment. I discovered then that some grown-ups couldn't dance. They'd shuffle round trying to waltz to everything, but if it were a waltz, completely miss the beat. The men were usually the worst, which led to exasperated women dancing together, bosom to bosom, taking it in turns to lead. But not my grown-ups! They danced as if it was as natural as breathing, the music coursing through them.

And over the years the wardrobe of wonderful dresses grew. Around the edge of the quilt there are small squares of dark green and gold taken from a dress my mother made when I was a teenager. Not so voluminous as those of a decade before, but still rich and beautiful. Mum was a wonderful seamstress. When I think of my parents together, they're always dancing, but there are countless other memories of my mother sitting over the sewing machine and it humming along as she fitted me out with frocks and dungarees, did all the extended family's alterations, and 'ran up' a dress for herself.

First, we would make a trip to the fabric section at the local department store and spend quite a time leafing through the pattern books to find something new. Then I trailed after her as she scrutinised the materials one by one, till finally the choice was made. Blue, rippled satin, black and bronze striped taffeta, a stretchy coffee-coloured jersey that "was a pest to sew" and never hung properly. Nearly all of them have found a place into the quilt

Stitched next to the dark green is my all-time childhood favourite; a pale ivory satin smothered in pink rosebuds with scattered green petals in raised stitch. I have only to look at it to see the pair of them doing their favourite slow foxtrot to the rhythm of 'Magic Moments' or 'Is You is or is You Ain't My Baby?', or jumping up when they heard the band start 'I Get a Kick Out of You.' "Oh, come on, it's a quickstep." How they could fly round, both so light on their feet, weaving skilfully around the shufflers, and carelessly throwing in complicated changes and flicks. I loved that fraction of a beat when they held, poised on their toes, before they each gave a little back kick just as the music came to that word in the title. A couple perfectly in tune.

Long before my father died, their dancing days had been reduced to the occasional family wedding, but the dresses hung in the spare wardrobe for years. I would riffle through them when I stayed, always regretting that I could never squeeze myself into any of them. Mum and I eventually began packing the dresses up ready to go to the Sense shop some years ago, but every time I could, I would salvage a beautiful remnant for the 'bit bag'. I knew I'd find a use for them one day.

When it was finished, the quilt had to go back home to my mother. She dozes in her armchair beside the fire now with it covering her sadly swollen and misshapen knees. Her hands are lying in her lap, their once tiny and nimble fingers bent and distended with the arthritis that courses through her. She will never dance or hand stitch a hem again, but I will always be able to picture her whirling happily round a dance floor with Dad. And when I catch her looking down at the bright squares and stroking them gently, I know she remembers too.

Finkle Street

Amanda Bird

There's an alleyway that runs between South Street and Finkle Street. I live on Finkle Street but I'm not from Cottingham, Hull or even Yorkshire. I've lived here nearly eleven years and the street has changed even in that decade, quite dramatically in some places. The woodworking shop at the western end, a maze of timbers of exotic colours and sheets of veneer in strange, smoky grains has gone and the building is a play centre for children. A family bought the building, converted it one hard-working summer and have made a thriving business. It is opposite a shop that once had pillars at the front and was a grocer's shop. The shop is long gone, and the front window filled with plywood so those who live there can watch television with only the ghostly fragrances of Lipton's loose leaf tea and bourbon biscuits to disturb them.

The alleyway opposite the play centre has seen much greater change – perhaps several hundred years. A map of 1775 shows the land along the length of Finkle Street neatly labelled with the names of owners: a Mr Burton, a Mr Ferraby and the evidently very wealthy Mr Watson. Where Finkle Street meets the centre of Cottingham, at Market or Town Green, the map shows a large garden or vegetable patch. The big houses face onto South Street. It is always more desirable to have the morning sun. Only the servants inhabit the kitchen, not the families of the big houses: the Gartons, the Bentons, the Everinghams. It hardly matters if the kitchens face north.

The 1775 map actually shows what is owned and rented out by just one man: the orchards and houses owned by Sam Watson, Esquire as the map refers to him. The alleyway borders an orchard that is rented out to a Mr Dixon who also rented the farm and farmhouse on the next plot. I try to imagine Finkle Street rich with apple and pear trees. Difficult!

The lines on the map fascinate me. I would guess the drawing formalises and makes real a short cut that people used for a very long time, before the map. The roads have not changed, of course not: Georgian Cottingham would be eminently navigable if dazzlingly rural to us. The green space fills up over the next hundred years with some grand houses built by the rich merchants of Hull who wanted to live in style, out of the city. Kevin McCloud would have loved them: "So, you're going to build a house on two and half acres of land in the centre of Cottingham, with a portico, stables and maids? Fascinating." History tends to love and revere those houses if not actually preserve them. I watched the tiles being thrown down for one of the few remaining grand houses on Newgate. The house was demolished so that the retirement flats could be built on the site. It is good that so many people have warm comfortable flats to live in where once there was one draughty Victorian edifice but nonetheless something is lost. But, I like the smaller houses like the terraced house I live in. Small from the front, it goes a long way back, to where the toilet and wash house would have been. Finkle Street is lined with terraced house built in phases as local builders bought land, erected houses, made profit and started all over again. They are good houses, if slipping a little with wear. Most still have their slate roof and some have their original door numbers. Great and small things that remind us we are not the first to live here, like the wallpaper we found in the rooms as we decorated. Floral pink behind a radiator, 1960s geometric behind the bath and trains from the 1950s in the middle bedroom.

The houses are private, even anonymous, hiding some wonderful histories. At the end of the terrace I live in is Roger's house. When Roger's parents bought the house it had been a company's headquarters and the double-fronted house had a telephone in every room, with yards of cabling. There were other surprises: the house had once been a wallpaper shop and some of the old sample books were buried in the garden, leaching their Victorian, arsenical greens into the soil.

Roger's house sits at the left hand end of the terrace. The prolific builder Whiting put up the elegant-fronted house by itself and people who bought it supposedly built four more houses beside it, for their daughters. In the Second World War, Nellists the fruit importers stored bananas and their wagon in the garage of the end house.

Whiting was one of the builders I mentioned, whose career seems to have spanned many decades and most of Finkle Street (numbers 87 to 97, 99, 107 to 117, 119 to 129, 131 to 141 and so on!) At the end of Roger's terrace is a driveway which gave access to what was the coal yard. On the opposite side is the police station with its curved window tops and large door. The station sergeant lived upstairs. The Inspector had the old police house opposite, much more spacious accommodation. The station was offices, then flats.

There was an orchard next to the police station, then more cottages. Land on Finkle Street was once used as a dumping ground for Hull's night soil. Maybe that explains the tall trees in most back gardens, the result of decades of the collected sewage of Hull being waggoned up the country road to Cottingham, to be spread on Finkle Street!

Orchard House is the other house on the street with a claim to grandeur. In the 1960s a family called Prince lived at the house. They had a grocers shop on Northgate. The family lost their daughter in a road accident and their son died of appendicitis. The story is a reminder that the street is about more than the houses: bricks and windows, chimneys and doors are only the backdrop to all the lives lived on the street. Stories for another day…

Another modern development: New Finkle Court that replaced barns and a big corrugated iron den that Roger and other children on the street played in. The open spaces must have been both irresistible and wildly enjoyable. Those spaces are gone, replaced by houses whose residents stare suspiciously at passers-by, put up locked gates and tell kids that the Court is private property.

Where the Court is was another garage. The owner used to race Porsches. There was another cycle shop. When that was burnt out, all that was salvaged, says Roger, was a Lotus car and a torch.

Past the Court, one of the cottages was a shop. A little old lady had a sweet shop there, then it was a dry cleaners. The next owner, a joiner, took out the shop window and rebuilt the front. It is impossible to tell that it was ever a shop. Between the cottages, down the alleyway, was a row of houses called Dales Buildings, condemned and demolished. Finally at the top of the street just before it turns onto West Green was the abattoir. Lorries full of squealing animals were brought in. Roger's Mum used to get lights (offal) for their cat. The land had to lie empty, decontaminating itself, for many years before it could be built on.

Finally, the chain pub the Fair Maid isn't on Finkle Street but Roger has one more story, too good to miss. The building (once a big house, then a club) was being renovated in the 1990s. Unfortunately, too many walls were knocked out and one day the whole back wall fell down. There was a radio that had been entertaining the builders on the roof and it played for days: it was too dangerous to take it down.

We are back to the alleyway at the western end of Finkle Street. I am staring down the length of the alleyway and wondering if I could, if I wished hard enough, walk its length and emerge next to the orchards of the eighteenth century, with trees in bloom. I wish I could.

Wilberforce, Blackburn & Sheaf

Ivor Church

To many, the title will sound like a firm of provincial solicitors; they are, in fact, three of the many buildings that make up the University of Hull.

If you look at the university website, it says the following: "As the 14th oldest English university, our compact and picturesque campuses encourage the traditional with modern facilities for staff and students…" It's not an idle boast; it *is* picturesque in parts – the gardens have won prizes and some of the buildings aren't too bad – or so I'm told.

My problem is that I don't understand the picturesque; I don't have the "chip" or the necessary piece of DNA. I've always been drawn … well, to give you an example…

When I was a child in the late 1960s, my father was involved in fitting out the new Terminal One at Heathrow Airport and this was seen – at governmental level – to be an opportunity to present British design to the world. All the most famous designers of the day were involved; money was no object. For reasons too tedious to explain, I didn't go to school much in those days and so spent many hours with dad as he wandered around this vast, empty building waxing lyrical about light-fittings, seating and carpets.

Now dad was a talented man and I loved him dearly, but God I was bored – I didn't give a toss about light-fittings, seating and carpets, I wanted to poke around the machine rooms. I wanted to look at the air-con fans. I wanted to see where the dustbin lorries parked.

Nothing much has changed; the only piece of décor that I really value in my house is a salvaged door from a Boeing 707 airplane, shipped at great cost from the USA.

My wife, I should add, is a saint.

Writing *Hull*

Almost fifty years later, last October to be precise, I came across a book called *Night and Day in W12* by Jack Robinson (actually a poet called Charles Boyle) in which photographs of Shepherd's Bush are accompanied by short prose pieces that begin in reality but often swerve away into urban myth… I was very taken by this, so I lovingly ripped it off, added my own interests in the backs and bowels of buildings and, well…in the last six months or so I have taken literally hundreds of photographs of Hull, planning – one day – to write about each…

Included here are three of these pieces, each inspired by a university building:

WILBERFORCE

Stairs were very big in 1960s architecture, as was textured concrete and windows that couldn't be adequately cleaned. The stairs, with their walkways and decks, formed a clash of right angles and diagonals. They promised much but often led nowhere other than an idea in an architect's mind.

I don't know who the architect was, although Denys Lasdun did a lot of universities at the time; he certainly did Leeds and that is much the same – linear, brutal with lots and lots of stairs. I don't know what he had in mind when he drew them; it could have been flow, or access – or that guy Escher, who did those etchings that twisted perspective into infinity and beyond.

These steps are dangerous as well as useless; their edges are sharp, their treads merge. No one uses them now, except to perch on in rare hot lunch breaks – to eat salad from Tupperware or read a few chapters of the latest blockbuster. Their greyness darkens. Rust appears as armatures leach. Litter gathers. The concrete, they say, is tired, "fatigued." There is talk of demolition. There is talk of a protection order.

At the base of the stairs is a little hut, painted red. Inside, sometimes, is a "real solicitor" hoping for clients; eager to sign them up before the ambulance arrives.

BLACKBURN

Perched up there, on the top of Robert Blackburn building, its windows striped, its structure stained, and its antennae stunted, it looks like the bridge of a concrete ship – the place from which the university is steered.

It looks abandoned, but that is merely a ploy; it is operational; it never sleeps.

Most people have never noticed it. The few that have probably assume that its purpose is scientific, possibly meteorological. Others, the conspiracy theorists, possibly see it as a watchtower…

None have guessed its true purpose, its function.

People, when they think of a university, imagine a Vice Chancellor to be in command - but he is merely a puppet, kept in check with a Professorship and a six-figure salary. The real power lies with those in the eyrie; they look down, counting students as sterling and plotting to kidnap the Vice Chancellors of the Russell Group of Universities.

They brood quietly – as does the building itself.

SHEAF

Like many children, I watched Dr Who from behind the sofa. I was scared of everything, especially the Auton's – animated shop dummies with conquering intent. I still sometimes walk past window displays and suddenly look back, convinced that a head was turned, a gesture made. It is my most graphic nightmare – well, one of several. And here they are again, staring out over tarmac and the girl's school, in hi-viz jackets and ill-fitting helmets – looking as if their power failed just as they set about smashing the glass. My wife tells me that they are obsolete mannequins, once used to train doctors and nurses, but I don't really believe her.

I've stopped walking that way to the car park.
I'm in the market for a machine gun.

References

Robinson, Jack (2007) Days and Nights in W12. London, CB Editions.

http://www2.hull.ac.uk/files/homepageBuildFeb/css/uniHomepage.html [Accessed 16 May 2012.]

Writing *Hull*

The Rank Outsider

Brian Lavery

Back when it seemed England was in black and white, it was a most unlikely movie mogul who was to bring a wave of new UK sex sirens crashing onto our screens.

Dismissed as a dunce by his tycoon father, J. Arthur Rank was destined for life at the family's city flour-mill in Holderness Road in the east of Hull.

Yet, this devout Christian would go on to become one of the saviours of British movies and founder of his own *School of Charm* to engender prodigious young talent.

In spite of his piety, he turned out sex bombs Joan Collins, Diana Dors and Kay Kendall and made them pin-ups. Not bad for a man who only entered the film industry to try to preach Christian family values to a wider audience.

J. Arthur, like Forrest Gump, was not a bright man. In fact, his biographer Michael Wakelin, described him as having "a certain intellectual dullness...that seemed to permeate his character." At its 1940s peak the Rank Organisation owned five studios – including Pinewood – and more than 650 cinemas, dwarfing many of its Hollywood rivals.

From its famous "golden-gong" opening sequence featuring the muscled body of British fighter 'Bombardier' Billy Wells, to its commitment to promoting young talent, the Organisation's impact on cinema has been far-reaching, even iconic. The *School of Charm* alone should secure J. Arthur's place in film history – it was the *Fame Academy* of its day (except its star pupils went on to enjoy actual success and had to have real talent in the first place). Without it, Christopher Lee's devilish Dracula or Joan Collins' not dissimilar *Dynasty* super-bitch, Alexis Carrington, may have never existed.

And Diana Dors may never have adorned many a teenage lad's wall in the 50s as the UK's Marilyn Monroe. J. Arthur was reputed to be fiercely protective of his young stars – glamour girls to the masses – they were guarded like convent girls by the studio.

Rank's commitment to independent filmmaking is equally celebrated – paying dividends with classics such as David Lean's *Brief Encounter*.

The unlikely story of J. Arthur Rank began in 1888. His father, Joseph, was already a successful flour merchant (of Rank Hovis fame) and staunch stalwart of the local Methodist circuit.

When his attempts in the flour business met a sticky end the by-then middle-aged J.Arthur busied himself showing Methodist films to church groups across the country, through his Religious Film Society.

With J.Arthur's obvious *trouble at t'mill*, it seemed that old Joseph's description of his off-spring as a daft lad proved that Rank senior was as good a judge of character as he was of baked goods.

Yet that Sunday School-inspired project was the bedrock for a multi-million-pound empire, which thrives still – albeit under US control. The seeds were sown when J. Arthur decided to try taking his films to a national audience in the early 1930s. After struggling to get the exposure he desired, with the zeal of a Biblical prophet he (with a little help from his friends) bought up studios, cinemas, acting schools and anything else he needed to spread the message.

It was a remarkable move, as critic Geoffrey Macnab explained in an entry for the *Encyclopaedia of British Cinema*: "In the early 1930s, his aim was no more ambitious than to use cinema as a vehicle for religious education in Sunday schools and Methodist Halls. In little under a decade, though, he was the most important figure in the British film industry." While early films, such as *Turn of the Tide*, maintained J. Arthur's Methodist themes, it wasn't long before the religious doctrine took a back seat to commercial interests – then came the prophet's profit. And by the early 1950s the Charm School was turning out talented, beautiful actresses to rival Hollywood's "blonde bombshells" - Marilyn Monroe, Jayne Mansfield and their ilk.

Old Joseph, not ten years in the grave, must have been turning like one of his old windmills. But, while he may have made the transition from Methodism to money-making, J. Arthur did not desert his Christian roots.

In 1953, he decided to plough his profits into the Rank Foundation charity, which still helps disadvantaged young people. A year earlier, after the death of his brother, he had returned to the family business, leaving the day-to-day running of the Rank Organisation to accountant John Davis.

It was the beginning of the end. By 1962, J. Arthur had severed all connections with the empire.

Today the company makes its money selling office equipment – a far cry from its glamour days of the 1940s and 50s.

As Geoffrey Macnab said: "In hindsight, it seems half comic, half tragic, that all Rank's efforts to set the British industry on its feet should spawn nothing more than a photocopying company and a leisure conglomerate."

The Charm School's graduates went their separate ways with varying degrees of success. Joan Collins waited until the 1980s to really make her mark – making an effortless transformation from English Rose to U.S. soap über-bitch. Christopher Lee is still an A-list actor to this day, winning plaudits for performances in the *Star Wars* and *Lord of the Rings* trilogies.

Diana Dors struggled through meningitis in the 1970s, before succumbing to cancer in 1984. After her funeral, her third husband reformed villain turned actor Alan Lake burned all her possessions and then shot himself to death some five months later.

Dors was, and still is, a British cultural icon – making the cut for the famous *Sgt. Pepper* album cover and later featuring in Adam Ant's *Prince Charming* video.

A year after her death she was featured in particularly poignant fashion on the cover of a CD by *The Smiths*.

Withernsea-born Kay Kendall, perhaps the most promising of the lot, died of leukaemia in 1959 aged just 32, shortly after marrying the actor Sir Rex Harrison.

J. Arthur Rank died in 1972.

Rank is commemorated at his former Holderness Road home in the city by a blue heritage plaque which was put there by the local council.

Hull Fair

Abby Harrison

As a young child my best friend, Heather, lived across the road. Whether this friendship was by accident or parental design I'm not sure, for our mothers were friends too. This meant the ordeal of Hull Fair could be shared between the two mothers. Going with someone my own age made parental accompaniment on rides superfluous and more rides could be experienced through joint nattering. Of course, joint saying 'no' also had an effect.

Heather was two and half months older than me and therefore her judgments were deemed more important in the relationship – especially when you were five. Also being born in August she had started school the year before me and was more knowledgeable. Her decisions on which rides to go on were tantamount to orders, but I was always happy to acquiesce; I thought Heather was fantastic.

One year, at about the age of five, we went to Hull Fair en masse: me and my mum, Heather, her mum and younger sister Mhairi. Mhairi, being two, was usually a nuisance we were forced to endure and play with, but she proved useful at the fair; being still in a pushchair she could plough the way through the crowds clearing a way for us to follow. We were told to hold on tight to the sides of the pushchair as the front wheels and Mhairi's feet did the hard work.

It was typical Hull Fair weather, a meteorological term in Hull: cold with enough rain to have made the field puddle-strewn. We'd had our fill of helter-skelters, riding the horses and dodgems, and had gazed in awe at the bigger rides we weren't yet allowed on, their ear-splitting music and accompanying screams something to look forward to when we were teenagers. I'd managed three games of the horse-racing game where you roll plastic balls towards holes of various points value to make your metal horse 'win' the race, winning every one and was closely clutching my prizes of a misshapen orange teddy, a colouring book and a Rubik's cube key ring. I still maintain that if the game were an Olympic sport I would be a gold-medal winner. We'd not quite had enough Hook-a-duck, which was impossible to have enough of. However, our mothers put a limit on winning two goldfish in little plastic bags each. The poor creatures never lived more than a week and just seemed to vanish from their bowls. It was much later I discovered my mum used to flush their dead bodies down the toilet before I saw them.

We had made our way back to the centre of Walton Street to the mecca of chips – Bob Carver's. Going to Bob Carver's at the end of the night, prior to buying those essential takeaway morsels of candy floss, brandy snap and toffee apples, was a ritual. The stall was always in the same place, midway along Walton Street, and strung with clear light bulbs. Bringing chips to the masses served with variations of fish or potato patties for the real starch-lover were its acne-ridden servers glistening with sweat (a sure sign of good greasy chips). Mushy peas also were dolloped out, although difficult to eat with paper, and getting a 'Styrofoam' tray was a "waste of money" and not for us. So plain chips it was, shared with the pecking fingers of mum who would swoop in unannounced and take the lovely squashy ones you'd been saving.

We positioned ourselves just behind the stall, away from the crush, to gobble down the burning chips. Mhairi was stuck proudly in front of us, nearest the warming barrel of hot cinders, kept quiet by the occasional descending chip from her mum. All was good in the chippy world and my thoughts had already strayed to the treats I would try and eke out from my mum on the walk back past the food stalls, when Mhairi started screaming. That wasn't so very unusual and I ignored it for some minutes, my eyes still drawn to the Hook-a-duck or the lights of the bigger rides I imagined my older brother being on. But Mhairi's screams were louder than usual and within a five metre radius actually blocked out the other fair noises.

"Hot chip" was the first suggestion for the cause and Mhairi's open mouth was bunged with her bottle of milk, but to no effect. She was wheeled further under the lights of Bob Carver's, the chip-hungry making way for the bellowing pram, and notice was finally taken of her little hand covering one tear-wet eye. Heather and I were still in a chip-induced stupor, but were dragged along in a wailing parade to the first aid portacabin further along Walton Street. The chips were gone now and across the stream of Hullitos rows of candy floss stalls drew our attention. Screams were still to be heard from the inside of the portacabin and before long the pram was out again and wheeling down the street and out of the fair. Our protests froze on our lips and for once Heather and I kept quiet as we trekked back to the car and drove to A and E, a rather unexpected turn to our night.

It turned out Mhairi had a little speck of hot cinder in her eye, but she was fine after an hour behind the scream-quivering cubicle curtain. Our hopes of returning for the sweet treats of Walton Street were quashed for that year, but we did get a flesh-coloured eye patch out of it.

Autumn in Hull was always special. Darkening nights brought not sadness at the end of summer but anticipation, where the first time you had to wear your glove elastic holster through your coat you celebrated instead of moaned and the appearance of toffee apples in the supermarket were derided as "not the real thing", because you knew it was coming. As it approached I started suggesting visiting usually forgotten relatives on the off-chance I could persuade them to take me to Hull Fair so I could go more than once. Kids with divorced parents suddenly gained kudos, for social standing in the September and October classroom was rated on how many times you were going. Three times was my record. And as the countdown dwindled to days gossip spread the school about how it was going to be bigger or smaller than last year, the new exciting rides, the best place to buy sweets and that waltzer ride with the missing bolt.

This year the fair returned with its crowds, endless food stalls and even more daring rides. I'm still an Olympian at the horse racing game, although the Hook-a Duck game no longer gives prizes of live fish. The first-aid portacabin is now a solid structure, but still resides in the same place. The fortune-tellers still bring in a great trade, although their traditional ornate caravans now are replaced by modern ones covered in photographs of the ladies with the almost-famous. I was delighted to see Gypsy Abigail still attended, someone I always wanted to visit, and was astonished to observe she didn't seem to have aged. Most surprising were the babies of the stall-holders sat proudly in their ginormous prams by the stalls, each child adorned by an elaborate lace and crochet bonnet, just as I remembered.

The smell of fried onions, sweet sweet toffee apples and candy floss, spilt beer and roasted chestnuts still brings a quickening of my breath as it hits my nostrils. Hull Fair is here.

Biographies

Amanda Bird - Amanda Bird, originally from the land of A.E. Housman, lived in four cities in three years but has finally settled in the East Riding. The life of a writer in Cottingham is generally serene and she has high hopes of getting some work done this year! Amanda found her MA in Creative Writing to be a fantastic experience that has always challenged and engaged her. She highly recommends it!

Nicholas Chapman - Nicholas Chapman currently lives in Stockton-On-Tees where he looks up in hope of being a Novelist.

Ivor Church - Ivor was a university lecturer for twenty-five years before realising that he didn't want to be a food scientist. Having written fiction for the majority of that time, he decided to grab the bull by the proverbial horns and try and get something published. With this in mind he took early retirement and enrolled in the MA Creative Writing at the University of Hull. He is currently writing a whodunit set in a typical English village of incomers, interest groups and empty drives. Being naturally pessimistic and fully aware of the challenges involved in selling a novel, he is also researching a book on civilian feeding in World War Two. His website is www.ivorchurch.co.uk

Kate Cooper – Kate says: "In the 1970s I came to Hull as a student of English and Drama for three years. Forty years on, I finally got round to taking my Creative Writing MA here. I believe in pacing myself! The years have been filled with teaching, (everything from nursery to sixth form, and including time working abroad,) travelling, reading voraciously and eclectically, and, since I gave up the day job, obsessive gardening. There have been some pretty ropey times on the health front along the way, but I count it all as valuable source material for the future. A personal guide to hospitals across the world could be a winner. I'm passionate about History, social history in particular, and it informs a lot of my writing. The piece included here, Foundations, is an example of my output in this genre, and gave me plenty of scope for researching through old documents and records, and discovering hidden connections. Sitting down with a pile of old books, black Bic poised over a notepad and laptop to hand, all alone, in complete silence - that's my idea of heaven. The second inclusion, Quilting the Light Fantastic, is a piece of memoir from my wonderful childhood in Margate, long before Tracey Emin and the Turner Centre re-discovered it, and conjures up happy family memories, not just of the parents it centres on, but aunts and uncles and cousins, a close-knit social hub. I have my own family here in Hull now, but the extended one 'down south' is an important part of who I am, and its values influence me still. I'm currently using more memoir, this time from my travels, to shape both some short stories and an extended piece of writing. Added research, as usual, will be vital. I feel the need to buy a plane ticket coming over me already, just thinking about it. There are places I haven't been yet. Who knows where writing will take me?"

Darren Lee Dobson - Darren Lee Dobson writes Sci-fi and fantasy fiction. He has lived in Hull for most of his life and owes the city a debt of gratitude for the inspiration it has given him in his writing. Originally trained as a Computer Programmer he has also worked as a Driving Instructor, teaching the good people of Hull safe driving standards. He holds a private pilot's licence and now lives in the East Riding of Yorkshire with his wife, Gladys. His first novel is expected to be completed by 2013.

Martin Goodman - Martin Goodman is Professor of Creative Writing at the University of Hull and Director of the Philip Larkin

Centre. He writes fiction and nonfiction. Check his website: http://www.MartinGoodman.com

Lorraine Gouland - Lorraine Gouland was born in a hotel in Somerset in 1965 and has been rootlessly floating about ever since – literally floating as she has spent much of the last thirty years at sea as a deck officer in the Merchant Navy. She has also worked with children in care and has recently gained an MA in Creative Writing from Hull University. A budding writer since the age of nine, Lorraine's work has appeared in The Coliseum Writers, Folio, Fresh Ink and Umber. She is still working at sea but when on leave she retires to her sister's garden shed to write and work on her blog Shedward http://lorrainesgouland.wordpress.com/

Mike Gower - After taking early retirement from a career that spanned roles as diverse as full-time firefighter, technical author, IT consultant, and corporate management jobs with titles as meaningless as the content, Mike Gower returned to his native East Yorkshire and took a Master of Arts in Creative Writing at the University of Hull. During the course he was a finalist in the 2010 GQ Norman Mailer Non-fiction Writing Competition. Mike's short fiction has been broadcast on BBC Local Radio, published in magazines and book-based collections, and won competitions – including the first ever Radio Humberside Short Story Competition back in 1990. In 2011, he designed and jointly compiled *Umber*, published by Umber Books in 2011 and available for free download at: http://cbpp.sanm.hull.ac.uk/index.php/umber/issue/view/22/

Abby Harrison - Abby Harrison was born in Hull and studied Politics and History at Lancaster University. Following post-university wilderness years working in numerous temp jobs and in Italy and Germany she trained to be a teacher. She completed the MA in Creative Writing at Hull University in 2012

Writing *Hull*

Brian Lavery - Brian is a writer, journalist, academic and teacher, living in Hull. The former national newspaperman returned to education in 2008 and has a first in English and Creative Writing from Hull University, where he is now reading for a PhD. His poetry and prose has been published by: Planet, Other Poetry, About Larkin and in the Umber anthology (2012). He is a regular performer with the Fresh Ink poetry group in the city. Brian lives in Hull with his wife Kath. They have two grown-up daughters, Catriona and Rose, aged 26 and 21, respectively.

Matthew Shaw - Matthew Shaw is 24 years old and has lived in Hull his whole life. He writes fiction, non-fiction and poetry, much of which is inspired by the local area.

Maria Stead - Maria says: "I am a 34 year old English teacher and have recently become a mother for the first time. I have taught and lived in Spain as well as in the UK. I enjoy writing about events and people in the past and creating fictional characters through whom to explore this world. I mix my memories with historical facts. I like to use different narrative voices to add levels of interest for the reader. Colour is also an important element for me in my writing to evoke a sense of place and to enliven character. Perhaps one of the most satisfying parts of the writing process for me is finding a metaphor that I feel captures the tone, movement and emotion of the piece. My own fond childhood memories of learning about Madame Clapham and her house meant that writing this piece was immensely enjoyable and hopefully a personal tribute to this formidable and gifted woman who brought haute couture to Hull."

David Tomlinson - David Tomlinson was a TV scriptwriter for twenty years, working with artists such as Mitchell & Webb, and Simon Pegg. He's published a number of anecdotal articles on TV, music, and travel, and a children's adaptation of 20,000 Leagues Under the Sea for Oxford University Press. He studied an MA in Creative Writing at Hull University, and claims his word order has improved, but his punctuation, still, leaves, something, to be desired. He's now working on his first young adult novel, and a non-fiction book about a guitar, a camper van and several years in therapy.

Steve Walsh - Winner of the Fathom Short Story Prize 2008, Steve Walsh is the author of several published and unpublished short stories. His short fiction has appeared in the Fathom 08 and Fathom 10 anthologies and Article magazine, published through North Lincolnshire's Fathom Press. In a parallel life as a public relations copywriter, he has also amassed a vast body of press releases, articles and case studies and seen at first hand the follies of PR at work in his home city of Hull. He currently divides his time between writing, looking after his son and avoiding doing any more corporate copywriting than he absolutely has to.

Chris Westoby - Chris Westoby is a new writer from Barton Upon Humber who enjoys colliding dark-voiced humour and farce with sincerity. Even his non-fiction is a study of how fact and experiences are bent by personal and public speculation and misinterpretation. Chris is currently writing his debut novel and a handful of short stories.

Alison Wood - Alison says: "Almost thirty years as a nurse has acquainted me well with the human condition. The art of nursing, the science of medicine and the written word belong together and I with them. Completion of the MA in Creative Writing has brought a continuation of my chosen theme of sexual health care and poetry. I have explored the actual, the factual, the fictional, the stereotypical, the experiential and the abstract of sexual health care and was commended in the 2012 Hippocrates Prize for Poetry and Medicine. Creative non-fiction fired me into a journalistic piece and I was honoured to be able to celebrate Boyes, a family firm within my community, capturing their contribution to Christmas festivities 2010 and a few shopping experiences. The Hull connection with Boyes was fascinating to discover. I have showcased at the Beverley Literature Festival and the Humber Mouth Festival and have read with Statement Drama Group. I do like to mix my poetry and sneak some humour in. Laughing has become very important with current NHS reform. Keep chins skyward, most of us are patients at some point in our lives."

Sarah Woods - Sarah Woods is a graduate of Hull University's MA in Creative Writing. She writes for both adults and children. Currently she is working on a Hull based novel dealing with debts, death and an audacious insurance scam. Originally from Wolverhampton, she moved to East Yorkshire 13 years ago. She is married with two daughters, a dog and a cat.